Identity and the New Psychoanalytic Explorations of Self-organization

Advances in science and the humanities have demonstrated the complexity of psychological, social, and neurological factors influencing identity. A contemporary discourse is needed to anchor the concepts required in speaking about identity in present-day understanding. In *Identity and the New Psychoanalytic Explorations of Self-organization*, Mardi Horowitz offers new ways of speaking about parts of self, explaining what causes a range of experiences from solidity in grounding the self to disturbances in a sense of identity.

The book covers many aspects of both the formation and the deconstruction of identity. Horowitz examines themes including:

- the sense of identity
- social learning
- biological learning
- identity and self-esteem
- levels of personality functioning and growth.

The book clarifies basic questions, defines useful terms, examines typical identity disturbances, and presents a biopsychosocial theory that explains how schemas operate in conscious and unconscious mental processing. The answers to the basic questions lead to improvements in psychotherapy practices as well as teaching and research methods.

Identity and the New Psychoanalytic Explorations of Self-organization will prove fascinating reading for those working in the fields of psychoanalysis, psychology, psychiatry, neuroscience, and the social disciplines.

Mardi Horowitz is Distinguished Professor of Psychiatry at the University of California, San Francisco, USA. He is former president of the San Francisco Center for Psychoanalysis and is the author of numerous articles and books.

PSYCHOLOGICAL ISSUES BOOK SERIES

DAVID WOLITZKY
Series Editor

Published by Routledge

Published by Jason Aronson

Published by International Universities Press

PSYCHOLOGICAL ISSUES BOOK SERIES

DAVID WOLITZKY
Series Editor

PSYCHOLOGICAL ISSUES BOOK SERIES

DAVID WOLITZKY
Series Editor

Identity and the New Psychoanalytic Explorations of Self-organization

Mardi Horowitz

Routledge
Taylor & Francis Group

LONDON AND NEW YORK

First published 2014
by Routledge
27 Church Road, Hove, East Sussex BN3 2FA

and by Routledge
711 Third Avenue, New York, NY 10017

Routledge is an imprint of the Taylor & Francis Group, an informa business

British Library Cataloguing in Publication Data
A catalogue record for this book is available from the British Library

Library of Congress Cataloging in Publication Data
Horowitz, Mardi Jon, 1934–
Identity and the new psychoanalytic: explorations of self-organization /
Mardi Horowitz.—First Edition.
pages cm
Includes bibliographical references and index.
1. Identity (Psychology) 2. Psychoanalysis. I. Title.
BF697.H575 2014
155.2—dc23
2013049587

ISBN: 978-0-415-73619-0 (hbk)
ISBN: 978-0-415-73620-6 (pbk)
ISBN: 978-1-315-77974-4 (ebk)

Typeset in Times
by Book Now Ltd, London

Printed and bound in the United States of America by
Edwards Brothers Malloy on sustainably sourced paper.

Contents

Illustrations

Figures

Tables

Foreword

Ever since Erik Erikson elaborated the conceptions of identity, identity formation and identity diffusion, as marking a major developmental milestone in the lifelong process of personality formation and maturation, imbricating in turn, in provisions and needs, with the successor generation, identity and its coherent formation or its varying deficiencies in formation, they have been a fundamental touchstone of psychoanalytic developmental theory. In this volume, Mardi Horowitz, whose professional life has been occupied with the study of personality growth and its intertwining with its deformations brought about by biologic handicaps and environmental traumatic vicissitudes and losses, has elected to synthesize his varying research themes through refracting character formation and its various malformations into illness development under the rubric of identity formation, ideally coherent and mature at its best, or impaired and disconnected, if unhappily or traumatically impacted.

This volume therefore encompasses the whole of normal development and the development of all the varieties of psychopathology and of illness formation, ranging from a coherent identity and a healthy self-esteem across the entire psychopathological spectrum from the almost normal neuroses of everyday life to the severest aberrations, the psychotically disorganized with what the author calls conflicted or disconnected identity and its extremes in severe narcissistic or malignant self-esteem. This is a way, not the usual way, but with telling vignettes that demonstrate a plausible way, to view the world of mental and emotional health and illness. And when viewing mental health and illness through the lens of the success, or not, of healthy, integrated and coherent identity formation and maintenance, the author seeks to provide the practicing clinician a guide to clinical therapeutic problems and ways to approach them in the ongoing clinical encounter.

Along the way, Dr. Horowitz separately devotes a three-chapter sequence to what he calls the "psychological learning of self-coherence," a focus on the internal developmental process and the central formative social experiences with the major family and other close caregivers and influences, followed by a chapter on "social learning and identity formation" with the focus on the wider social-cultural surroundings, the space and time within which one grows and with which one is influenced to fit or not, happily or less so, but always formatively, and, finally, the third chapter of this trio, the biological genetic coding that helps determine the direction and the physiological and behavioral limits of the evolving personality. The three chapters together present the overall summation of possibilities, influences, and pressures that interactively fashion the ultimate successful achievement, or not, of a secure, coherent, and healthy identity that is the desired outcome that this author hopes he can help the reader, or the successful psychotherapy patient, achieve.

Basically what the book thus offers is a variant way to view the overall human condition and its vicissitudes, using identity and its formation and deformations as the central looking glass, and this hopefully will prepare you to measure for yourself, the new value you find with this new psychoanalytic perspective on human mental and emotional health and illness. It provides such a fresh perspective for me. I trust that it does the same for you.

Robert S. Wallerstein, MD

Preface

We are going beyond Descartes' famous phrase: "I think, therefore I am (cogito, ergo sum)." The "I" in that phrase was considerably subdivided into complex concepts in the new knowledge attained from psychoanalytic, psychological, social, and neuroscience studies of the last century. This monograph is part of a *Psychological Issues* series that, in its early monographs, emphasized persisting mysteries of self-organization, most notably by the focus of Erik Erikson on identity formation as a series of developmental milestones, ones that could have normal or abnormal maturational possibilities. I intended this monograph to continue that kind of work, examining contemporary psychological, social, and neuroscience points of view, and, as he and Piaget did, considering unconscious as well as conscious mental processes.

Through decades as a psychoanalyst, psychotherapist, researcher, and professor of psychiatry, I have analyzed personality growth as it intertwines with posttraumatic stress disorder and with the often harsh process of mourning the loss of significant loved ones (Horowitz, 2011, 2014). These studies focused my attention on dissociation, decomposition in self-organization and, for some subjects, formation of an enhanced identity. A multiplicity of possible self-states made singular definitions of identity misleading at best.

Selves: the multiplicity problem

Multiple self-states can be observed in most people when they report their innermost experiences. As we examine both the intrapsychic and the interpersonal world in which minds form and endure, the issue of multiplicity breaks down into five related potential discords about what "identity" means:

1   People experience frequent *discords between their internal sense of who they are and the reflection*s of themselves provided by their surrounding social connections.
2   People have expressive patterns that lead observers to find that they seem to have *divisions between conscious and unconscious meanings as organized into their attitudes about self and relationships.* For example, a man may

believe himself to be caring, loving, and trustworthy, but his unconsciously driven actions betray to observers a side of his identity he does not want to see—a readiness to betray others or get redress on long past grievances.

3   People often find within their own minds *identity manifestations that are multifaceted, discontinuous, and not what they desire.* Most people desire a sense of "true self" that will maintain continuity over time. However, multiple self-states may alternate, leaving a sense of uncertainty about what to expect next.

4   People may experience a discord between *their need to preserve a lifelong sense of identity continuity and the need to realistically understand major changes in their bodily self, such as those of aging and disability, and loss of attachments, as in the death of a lifelong marital partner.* The realities of aging may create discontinuities in both internal self-experience and social self-presentation. The aging person in question may behave strangely, perhaps dressing "too young." A person long grounded in solid self-coherence may seem to fragment as an early sign of a dementing process, or as a regressive response to loss of a close community or job.

5   People often define themselves by referring to their continuity of values, yet they seem to have value conflicts as, over time, they struggle with multiple values from multiple social inputs. Mobility and rapid societal changes especially exacerbate the multiplicity issue. The most frequent discords, ones in need of some type of harmonization in order to achieve higher levels of personality functioning, are *between personal goals for satisfaction and the social surrounding world that has rules for ethical living. These conflicts lead to serious lapses in respect and self-esteem if responsible compromises are not achieved.*

This book asks questions and offers answers in its series of chapters. Chapter 1 provides some terminology for us to use as we address, with some shared definitions, the open issues on identity theory. Chapter 2 illustrates frequent yet extreme experiences of disturbances to an inner sense of identity. Chapters 3–5 take that terminology and those observations of identity disturbances in the direction of explanation. The questions we want to answer with better theories are summarized at the beginning of Chapter 3, which then lays out a psychological and developmental theory of self organization. Chapters 4 and 5 successively add social and neuroscience perspectives on what influences the intrapsychic formation of self and other attitudes, beliefs, roles, and values, as well as practices of expression of ideas and emotions.

The final third of the book applies an integrative self-organizational theory to the implications for clinically relevant action. Chapter 6 examines disturbed personality functioning in terms of assessing and reacting clinically to levels of self–other schematic capacities of patients. Chapter 7 considers the application of identity and self-organizational theory to clinical work with several typologies of personality disorder. Chapter 8 considers the issue of narcissistic psychopathology versus healthy self-esteem. Chapter 9 explores growth of identity even after dire events, such as the loss of a loved one. It serves as a review of the possibilities for self re-definition.

The Appendix applies these concepts to research methodology. Please notice that a glossary of terms is also provided. That glossary may help with understanding terms at any time during your reading. You have permission to copy and distribute it for use in teaching.

References

Horowitz, M. J. (2011). *Stress response syndromes* (5th ed.). Northvale, NJ: Jason Aronson.

Horowitz, M. J. (2014). Grieving: The role of self representation. *Psychodynamic Psychiatry, 42,* 89–98.

Acknowledgments

I wish to thank Zachary Vanderbilt, Marilyn Spoja, Jaimee Marchetti, and Masha Brown for their literature research and manuscript preparation. Renee Binder, Robert Hendren, Lowell Tong, Virginia Sturm, Zachary Vanderbilt, and Anna Glezer added concepts to key chapters. Research was essential to this work, and that background was supported by excellent awards from the National Institute of Mental Health and the John D. and Catherine T. MacArthur Foundation. I am especially grateful to Robert Wallerstein for the Foreword, David Wolitsky for guiding the early drafts towards publication in this series, Kate Hawes, Kirsten Buchanan, Susannah Frearson and the staff of Routledge for making this manuscript see the light of the printed book.

Chapter 1

Questioning identity

Societies that surround individuals define the *identity* of a person as being the fact of being that person, usually as a bodily entity, perhaps as that person's perceived roles within the society. If the police heard that someone reported that I stole money from the market, I would say it was a case of mistaken identity. I am innocent, a respected professor, and not the perpetrator whom I must admit looked like me on a surveillance camera.

In the social system, I am that body that contains just me and no one else. My DNA can prove it. But inside my mind I am not always so clear about my *sense of identity*. It is this inner variation of multiple self-states that leads us to analyze parts of self and, as teachers or clinicians, to seek effective ways to help people toward greater coherence between them.

Self-esteem, identity diffusion, and lifetime efforts at self re-definition are common issues. During the 1992 U.S. Presidential election, Vice-Admiral James Stockdale was a largely unknown Reform Party candidate for Vice President. In his televised debut, he was to debate Republican and Democratic opponents. Stockdale introduced himself with the opening remark "Who am I, and why am I here?" and, to his visible embarrassment, the audience laughed.

What he may have meant to say was, "When I tell you my history, you will know who I am and you will know the principles on which I stand." The big surprise was that some—those who laughed at his comment—understood his remarks as meaning "I stand before you, uncertain about my identity and my worthiness." Why did he get that response from the audience? Some felt an empathetic resonance, because most people have moments of uncertainty and discomfort about their personal identity.

Identity is questioned biologically, socially, and psychologically as in studies of blood-lines, ethnicity, and internal sense of cultural belonging. The political and often economic problem is this: are you the person you say you are or the person we say you are? A case in point is a recent debate concerning Native American heritage and a personal sense of identity as being rooted in a traditional culture. The case was that of a candidate for a Massachusetts Senate seat, Elizabeth Warren, a Harvard Law School professor. She was listed as a Native American in several law school directories. Her opponent's campaign used this fact to attack her character by implying that she was an opportunist who lied about her indigenous people's identity, since, the opponent said, Warren was not a blood-line Native American. Warren's "proof" of her identity was, "My mother told me so," a family legacy of meaningful connections with traditions and certain cultural values.

Some tribal registries require a "blood quantum" of ancestry, but other tribes indicate that Native American identity is something a person can claim for him- or herself, that one may choose how to relate oneself to a sharable culture. Warren was not seeking social advantages for herself on the basis of her Native American identity claim. However, her place of employment—Harvard University School of Law—did seek advantage, counting Warren as a Native American lent the department a legitimacy in conforming to requirements to show faculty diversity (see the stories in the *Washington Post* and the *New York Times*, 2012).

Oscillating external and internal points of view

Suppose a man identifies himself, and is identified by others, as "a writer" and as one who has written many things over a long time. Many critics and his family have called him: "a fine writer." He liked that role for his identity and self-definition: he said within his mind, enjoying a bit of self-esteem, "I am a fine writer."

He had published a prize-winning short story a few years ago. Now he was writing another short story, but this time it was not going well. He felt that the short story in process would be rejected unless he received better inspiration and wrote better sentences. Because he is a fine writer—that is, his sense of identity in some self-states—he expects that he might eventually have such inspiration and revise the current mediocre draft into an excellent short story. If he possesses a solidity and continuity of his sense of identity that sustains him through his work, he will rise to meet the challenge, feeling self-confident.

In contrast, consider the commonplace self-doubts of creative people. Perhaps this writer has so much doubt that he can no longer hold onto this identity commitment of having been, being, and becoming once more, a fine writer. He always wondered where his inspiration came from. He felt that he was not in control of "his muse." He wondered: does his creative part even reside inside his mind? If inside, why is "it"—that part of himself—sometimes uncooperative? Was he in different states of mind—inspired and not inspired, for example—sometimes brilliant, sometimes competent, sometimes sluggish and incompetent?

The doubts of the writer help me to illustrate how self-states can fluctuate from time to time. Metaphorically, the fluctuation is also from place to place, as if complexes of self-beliefs occupy different spaces in the theater of his mind, looking out at his drafts and imagined readers from different points of view, arriving at different appraisals, from promising to dooming. The important additional factor is his level of reflective self-observation. The writer may or may not have an over-arching view of multiple selves, fluctuating in time and mental space, all as parts of his overall self-organization and ongoing identity. If he has an overarching, *supraordinate self-schema,* and it is activated, then a consciously self-reflective agency helps him understand his fluctuations of mood and attitude. This higher capacity for self-reflection on aspects of self can ameliorate the sense of doubt, preserving morale and energy over times of critical appraisal of his productivity. The higher capacity regulates attention, and that control of attention ameliorates self-conscious emotional potential such as shame or fear of social embarrassment.

The self contained in and reflected by communities

Others may observe the writer. They may have their own ways to categorize his mind. They may have a theory that allows them to know that the writer may be in alternative states, and that he may even go through cycles of states, going from initial inspiration, into self-doubting, and then to exhilaration over his work product. The other persons might think the writer seemed vain and exhibitionistic in his exhilarated state and timidly uncertain, asking for guidance, in his doubting state.

Such observers might even form character judgments, perhaps gossiping at a party while he was out of earshot. They might agree that he was a charming but vain narcissist; he was a pleasure to converse with, but he could not be trusted to remain reliable as a friend. That would be different from agreeing that he was compulsively self-doubting and a very reliable friend. An acquaintance might even comment on him as having one identity, fine writer, while believing inwardly he had another identity, a has-been.

Inner identity is different from identity as reflected in the eyes of the beholders that surround the individual, actually, and in his mind. Entering the room, the writer felt like a writer because the guests knew his works and reputation, and they looked at him with respect. Before he came in, though, his self-esteem was low because he had doubts in his current skill to create future works. He anticipated he would feel embarrassed because he expected to be overlooked and ignored. He sensed the admiring looks from others and soon felt good, even excited. Little did he know that behind the smiling faces, some of the people thought the writer had become a bit foolish, perhaps to be pitied where he once was envied.

Defining our terms

The *Oxford English Dictionary* says the word *identity* comes from the Latin term *identitat,* which means, "It is the same." The main definition reads "The sameness of a person or thing at all times or in all circumstances; the condition of being a single individual; the fact that a person or thing is itself and not something else; individuality, personality." Here, the dictionary writers have emphasized identity from an external point of view, the social assessment that the identity of a person is acknowledged by how others perceive distinguishing characteristics.

Of course, people often worry, when they think about their identity, how they are perceived and interpreted by others. And their mind has been formed in social frameworks, even their brains were formed from social evolutionary forces and epigenetics. Inside the person, self-beliefs and attributes exist, and judgments by others may be formulated. The person may vary in self-state because of which others are now reflecting, or perceived as reflecting, the self. That person's internal formulation may not match what other people actually think and feel. People vary in degrees of accuracy in their appraisals of what others are thinking about them. Projective errors are rampant. And people vary in their reflective self-appraisals, their ability to comprehend discords, to harmonize them, and to re-define self.

These ambiguities in observing identity are noted in the subordinate definitions of the *Oxford English Dictionary*. *OED* notes self as, "a permanent subject of successive and varying states of consciousness. Self also signifies a collection of traits and dispositions that constitute one of various conflicting personalities within a human being." We will address those conflicting personalities. We are going to consider parts of the self and how well they do or do not cohere or configure together as central, organizing schematizations (Harter, 2012).

We'll need some words to think of components—parts of self that may be configured together or not—rather than of one bodily entity as seen externally. That is why hyphenated words about self are often found in cognitive science. One such term is *self-schema*, which means unconscious as well as systematized generalizations about the self. Related terms are *self-belief*, or *self-concept*, but these terms imply consciousness and schemas operate pre-consciously to organize mental states. This book will tend to use the word *self-representation* to refer to conscious and communicative expressions.

The word *schema* implies a kind of cognitive map, so that a self-schema is an organized configuration of information coded in memory, probably as associational linkages across many modalities of the brain's memory encoding systems. A *self-state* is a condition organized by the activation of a particular self-schema, leading to self-representations, and so, to a sense of identity in consciousness and how one is separate from while attached to others.

Self-organization refers to the overall assembly of self-schemas. *Self-representation* refers to a conscious belief about the self. This terminology allows us to examine complex and hierarchical organizations of *self-states*.

Self-schemas are configurations of subordinate meanings, and *self-organization* is a larger linked configuration of self-schemas. Between self-schemas and self-organization might be several *supra-ordinate self-schemas* that cluster a group of self-schemas but perhaps are dissociated from other supra-ordinate configurations. *Self-coherence* is a quality of overall functioning of self-organization in that an individual may associate or segregate (dis-associate) multiple self-schemas.

Conscious and unconscious mental processes

A conscious sense of identity, the self-observing processes of self-appraisals, and the values used to contrast an ideal with an actual here-and-now self, these are all determined by unconscious mental processes, which in turn depend on brain capacity and activity as well as social contexts of immediacy. These processes are organized by unconscious meanings such as schemas of self and others, which in turn depend on what has been learned and socially reinforced or at least reflected back on the person in past experiences, experiences now deposited and generalized in many memory systems. Identity to be sensed as a self, as a me, as an I of continued vitality, requires complex connectivities of memory systems.

There is a lot that can "go wrong." That is why identity is sometimes disturbed, fragmented, or absent in an alarming sense of depersonalization. A person may, socially, fake self-presentation as if feeling competent and confident, while inside feeling like an imposter.

Self-observation

With self-reflective awareness, a person may notice that some self-states feel discordant with other self-states. These differences in the sense of identity are usually due to some kind of mismatch between sets of information pertaining to the self. The mismatch may be within unconscious mental processing, assessing contradictions between associational networks. The result of a mismatch can activate emotional systems, and these self-conscious emotions may be felt without clear reasoning about why they have arisen, or why a mood may persist in spite of efforts to rouse oneself from it.

Research indicates that the most frequent mismatch is in the contents of appraisal of the physical self. When looking in the mirror one may feel that one's skin color, hair quality, or a facial feature is not in accord with expectation. This mismatch, if negative in emotional response says, in effect, I don't like my looks. The degree of experienced disturbance in these self-appraisals is variable. Consider the difference between unconscious appraisals that might be put down as words such as, "Oh, I am having a bad hair day" and "I will forever have substandard hair because of my genetic inferiority."

Any mismatch between real and "ought-to-be" self-images can give rise to complex feelings such as shame. For example, looking in my mirror, I could think, in effect, "Because my head is bald, I am ashamed that people might perceive me as old and unattractive." If I expected to see an ugly old guy in the mirror and that expectation was mismatched with a perception that I actually looked pretty good, then I could feel consciously proud that I have aged gracefully and have remained attractive but in a different way than when I was younger. If I unconsciously expected to see a handsome young man, and I see a bald guy with a lot of wrinkles, then I might feel dismay. A positive mismatch leads to positive feelings, augmenting self-esteem, "Wow, I look better than I anticipated," and a negative mismatch leads to distress, diminishing self-esteem: "Wow, not as attractive as I expected." The feelings may be conscious, and at least some of the reasons may be unconscious.

Enhancing self-observational capacity allows some people to think more broadly and openly about what they want, what they value, what they could do, and what they fear. Such self-observation is a common tool for personality growth. It allows a person to compare and contrast beliefs, modify attitudes, and bring conflicting parts of self into better harmonization. In such a context, a relative split between the *experiencing self* on the one hand and the *observing self* on the other hand allows a person to compare alternative and conflicting views, and perhaps forge new self-definitions.

Self-states contained in inner working models of relationships

People may be more consciously aware of their feelings, and their attitudes about relationships with others than they are aware of the parts of self that go into the presence, absesnce, or distortion of their sense of identity. This is reasonable because the conscious mind is predicting what can happen next, and social engagements are very important. Self-schemas are contained in mental maps of relationship: the self as having roles in transaction with others as having roles in regard to the self.

These cognitive schemas of attachment and connectivity contain and cause intuitive attitudes about self and other. The cognitive maps for possible relationships, for expectations and for organizing intentions, contain information that has been generalized from past interactions (Bowlby, 1969; Stern, 1985; Horowitz, 1991; Baldwin, 1992; Ryle, 1997; Young, Klosko, & Weishaar, 2003). These inner maps operate to organize unconscious mental processes. These unconscious meaning structures persist, leading to continuities in attachment. These self and other schematizations not only persist, they also slowly change, as while, for example, mourning the loss of an attachment.

While largely unconscious, the self and other attitudes contained in *role-relationship models* can possibly be brought to conscious awareness by verbal or pictorial representation (Bucci, 1997; Horowitz, 1998). These representations enable self-observation. The reflective and conscious stream of self-awareness can then modify the generalized attitudes. Alterations in self–other schemas can then alter self-states and a sense of identity (Horowitz, 2005).

For example, a person may recall a memory involving an insult. Reliving the memory in the mind still hurts. Reappraisal of who did what, how, and why leads to revised understanding of intentions and expectations. Each repetition of the appraisal can lead toward developing a plan for how to avoid or how to respond optimally to future encounters.

Such processes can help the person form new beliefs about the self and other, and plans for new action. New behaviors and interpersonal experiences can alter experience and such important feelings as self-esteem.

While a core technique in insight-promoting psychotherapies, experienced clinicians have learned that self-observational discoveries can be hazardous for some people, especially those with more disturbed levels of personality functioning (Vasire & Wilson, 2012). For example, some people seek avenues of insight or so-called mind expansion because they want to find their true self, imagining a true self that is spiritually pure and shining, hoping that it will come forth into the conscious mind from the external universe or emerge from within, from previously unconscious locations.

Instead of a rosy picture of a perfect "true self," the seeker of a single core self may find instead sets of severe contradictions. Uncovering beliefs that usually operate unconsciously, a person may discover intentions that would lead to conflicting goals, wishes that are knotted together with fears of the consequences, and so also coupled to avoidances of thinking about or acting upon the wishes. The person may discover inner motives that contain, perhaps, brutal urges to hurt others as well as wishes to preserve compassionate connections. The person, while placing a value on compassion, may find within himself discordant values of self-promotion, with intentions that are entirely self-serving, and anticipate that under certain circumstances he might choose to act at the expense of others.

Such recognitions of conflicts in values, and discrepancies between desired and perceived self-concepts can lead to intense anxiety, depression, and self-loathing. Bad ideas can be projected outward from self as a defensive stance to avoid such negative moods. The person inwardly interprets an interpersonal situation erroneously as if hostility, for example, stemmed from others and not the self. If such defenses fail, then dysregulation of emotion can lead to states of mind characterized by disorganized thought and fragmented, diffuse, and quite negative identity experiences.

We may conclude that intrapsychic self-organization is not the same as a current sense of conscious and reportable identity, which stems from a conscious self-reflection about self-concepts. This internal conscious sense of identity is influenced by a conscious sense of how one is being reflected by the opinions and actions of others. Unconscious mental processes influence both. These unconscious processes have considerable complexity.

As shown in Figure 1.1, each individual has a latent repertoire which has multiple self-schemas. Different ones of these may be currently activated or left latent. The result is a variety of possible self-states. The transactive influences of conscious on unconscious, and unconscious on conscious mental processes are illustrated by the arrows in Figure 1.1.

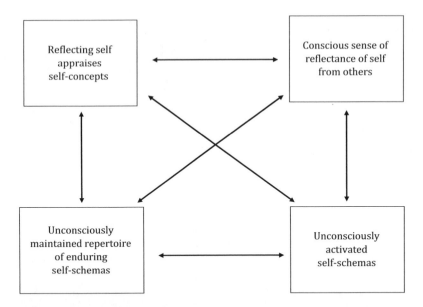

Figure 1.1 Interactions of levels of awareness on self-organization

An unconscious repertoire of self-schemas will have been derived from generalizations of memories of past experiences. Current social and mind/brain processes, including how others are reacting to or ignoring the self, may differentially activate elements of the repertoire. Different activations can organize information differently in different self-states. Some self-states become the clinically important disturbances in a conscious sense of identity, as illustrated in Chapter 2.

Identity disturbances

Identity disturbances are conscious experiences about self-definition that can impair one's ability to lead a satisfying life. One of the aims of this chapter is to ask specific questions about how and why these disturbances, in varied forms, occur. That will help us to understand the differences in mental functioning between self-states containing a sense of identity disturbance and self-states that contain a conscious sense of identity coherence, as well as a range in between.

Psychotic spectrum disorders

The most severe disturbances of identity occur in the psychotic spectrum of psychiatric disorders. A person's irrational self–other beliefs may be represented consciously in delusions and hallucinations. Such symptoms depart from reality; the self may be composed of mixed-up characteristics of others. The person may fail to accurately distinguish all bodily parts as belonging to the self. Some symptoms involve merging of self with others or with objects. A sense of alien invasion may occur, as in the sense of demonic possession of the bodily self.

In a review of the Austen Riggs Center's careful records of 226 psychiatrically hospitalized patients, severe childhood trauma was noted to be surprisingly frequent as the source of the mental contents repeated as re-enactments involving identity disturbances (Drapeau & Perry, 2004). Dissociation between experiences of different self-states led to the appearance of the patient's having fragmented self-organization. For some treatment-resistant psychotic patients, a lack of improvement was correlated with the patient's loss of a sense of self as the agent for making choices of bodily actions (Fromm, 2006).

In his intensive psychoanalytically oriented treatment of patients with psychotic experiences, Ogden (1992) noted that they often reported streams of quasi-somaticized sensations and emotions as pure experiences, like a perceptual flow of images (including auditory images in words). These pure experiences seemed to come without thought or self-awareness, without the kinds of reflective, conscious functioning that would recognize oneself as the one having these flows of sensory thoughts. In some psychoanalytic observations, this is called: concrete thinking without symbolic thinking (Bion, 1997; Fonagy, Gyorgy,

Jurist, & Target, 2000). Ogden found that some patients developed a paradoxical response, as they progressed. As they gradually developed more sense of self as thinker and experiencer, they became more anxious, as if the self was in danger because its disturbances could now be noticed by itself. Bromberg (2003) replicated such observations, calling the disturbed identity experiences "disconnected self-states." The theory put forth in Chapters 3–5 of this book attempts to provide an understanding of such disconnections, as well as an explanation of how optimum brain connectivity may occur.

Borderline personality disorder

Borderline personality disorder is described as a pattern of mood instability, tumultuous and unstable relationships, an extreme fear of—and frantic efforts to avoid—abandonment, as well as possible self-destructive tendencies. This disorder may include experiencing periodic states of mind in which, instead of a stable sense of identity, the person may have a distressing sense of emptiness and confusion about what is real, what is fantasy, and who one really is. Such experiences, and some other symptoms of this disorder, may overlap with a provisional diagnosis of Complex PTSD (Posttraumatic Stress Disorder), complex because there are still disturbances from childhood traumas as well as more immediate, adult, traumatic episodes (Gunderson & Sabo, 1993).

Under stress, a person with borderline personality disorder may develop extreme and dissociated binary thinking, identifying his or herself as either all good or all bad. This binary split leads to a very painful emotional experience and a difficult-to-manage cognitive interpretation of the world. The person, in the most regressive states, acts as if two impossible-to-reconcile parts of the self are at odds with one another. Self-loathing can occur, which may be why, when added to a loss of hope, episodic impulses toward self-destruction are common. More frequently, a patient feeling abandonment by the therapist may storm out of the office enraged, threatening suicide. Instead of suicide, self-cutting episodes may occur.

An act of cutting the self, as in slashing a forearm, may appear as a puzzling symptom of crisis because it looks like self-harming or suicidality. The reason for puzzlement may be that the painful action—instead of leading to high distress—may actually lead to a sense of restored identity coherence. That is, self-cutting can momentarily relieve a distressing sense of identity emptiness and self-state chaos because the self is, in a way, controlling the self by regaining life-affirming sensations, and perhaps getting help—as in going for sutures to an emergency room. The identity-diffusing emotional state can be reduced by a soothing connection to a caring other.

Extended therapy can reduce these disturbances in favor of identity cohesion, and the prognosis is good for improving the level of self-schematization through personality growth (Linehan et al., 1993; Fonagy et al., 2000; Young, Klosko, & Weishaar, 2003; Clarkin, Yeomans, & Kernberg, 2006; Kernberg, 2009; Gabbard

& Horowitz, 2010). A theory of dissociation and coherences in self-organization is needed to account for both such disturbances and such advances.

Binary self-states in other personality disorders

An important aspect of personality disorders is that they repeat maladaptive patterns in spite of new social learning opportunities. These patterns involve identity and relationship attitudes. Due to developmental coping with problems in identity and roles of relationship with others, the patterns often involve combinations of wished-for and dreaded selves, a problem of multiple self-conceptualizations that, for brevity, we are calling *binary self-state potentials and limitations*. In the borderline, the all-good self-state has the advantage of self-esteem, but when it cannot be stabilized there may be an explosive shift to an all-bad self-state, with seemingly no self-attributions in between.

Binary self-states refer to opposites in identity experiences, that is, seemingly oppositional self-definitions within one person. The dichotomy in histrionic disorder is often passive and active; in compulsive disorder, it is dominant and submissive selves in relation to others; and in narcissistic personality disorder, there may be a splitting or segregation of attributes of a grandiose self-schematization and an enfeebled, weak self-schematization.

Histrionic personality disorder is characterized by a pattern of excessive emotionality, attention seeking, and dramatization, including an excessive need for approval and inappropriately seductive behavior (American Psychiatric Association, 2013). People with this personality style are usually thought of as lively, dramatic, vivacious, enthusiastic, and flirtatious. When social functioning is impaired, however, the excessively dramatic turns demanding, with surprisingly variable shifts from intense positive to intense negative emotionality. This style of relating, while it does attract attention, becomes an obstacle to meeting life's challenges.

As just mentioned, a person with histrionic personality disorder may have seemingly binary self-states in which one very active self acts dramatically to gain attention, perhaps alternating with very passive, or seemingly shy, self-presentation (Horowitz & Lerner, 2010). An identity dilemma is prominent in the juxtapositions, within the relationships and self-occupancy of those roles. Traits of extreme passivity seem more authentic internally while behaviors of self-exhibition garner attention, but feel inwardly inauthentic.

Such dilemmas of seemingly opposite but enduring self-schemas may also be noted in *obsessive-compulsive personality disorder*. Self-states may oscillate in a maladaptive fashion, between strong and weak polar positions. The strong and domineering self-state can harm others by attempts to control relationships, whereas a shift to an unassertive and submissive self-state can undo the over-control at the expense of enlightened self-interest. A disorder is present because synthesis into an overall self-organization has never occurred. Self-identity theory should explain how learning can lead to harmony of these polarities: oscillating between being too strong and controlling, and being too weak and fearing being controlled. As self-organization is advanced toward harmony, the person with the disorder stops undoing too strong with too weak, too weak with too strong, and learns to cooperate from a grounded center of self-solidity and cooperative mutuality. Our theory should account for how to understand the initial formulations and the adaptive changes leading toward coherence in self-states.

The hallmarks of *narcissistic personality disorder* include a preoccupation with power, status, vanity, entitlement, and resulting grandiosity. The self-state can present a "great" or "enfeebled" binary of self. Individuals with this disorder can be extremely self-absorbed and sensitive to criticism. They have difficulty understanding the feelings of others. The social presentation of the shame-riddled self is quite different from the sometimes charming or charismatic, grandiose self. The person experiences and manifests a lack of coherence between self-states organized by idealized self-schemas, and deflated self-schemas (Horowitz, 2012). Our theory will have to account for how defensive motivations can accomplish a binary-type shift from an irrationally inferior self to an equally irrational superior self. It should also address how attempts to stabilize the superior self-schema function as an unconscious defensive operation to avoid searing shame.

There are other disorders of personality, and disturbances in identity in a variety of personality styles. The ones explained in this book have to do with *either-or* self-states. Our theory will explore flexible, coherent, and self-as-the-same experiences as they occur in relatively undisturbed people who know themselves across their own different states of mind. Our theory will also look at the more disturbed personality functioning in which the kind of problematic binaries of seemingly opposite views of self that we have just discussed occur with less coherence in attitudes across varying states of mind. Such people express views, which seem to function as segregated self-attitudes that blossom into different self and relationship patterns, puzzling their close friends and relatives or work partners, and preventing a continuous sense of identity consolidation.

Major depressive disorder

Major depressive disorder (MDD) consists of a negative mood, loss of self-esteem, and loss of ability to experience normal satisfactions and pleasures (American Psychiatric Association, 2013). Self-states similar to self-representational deflations in narcissistic personality disorder may occur. Hopelessness for the self in the future may be a characteristic, and can contribute to suicidality if and when such ideation occurs.

During recurrent episodes, a patient reports degraded identity experiences such as "I am a worthless person." With remission, rational self-regard returns. With relapse, the same degraded self-concepts may seem reactivated. Similar phenomena may occur in some patients with bipolar affective disorders. Degraded, hopeless self-representations intrude into awareness in depressive episodes and contrast with grandiose self-attributions that can occur with a switch into manic or hypomanic states. Irrational, positive beliefs about self may return with each cycling into a manic or hypomanic state. Self-identity theory should explain unconscious retention of the same, irrational self-beliefs that seem to leave, disappear, and then reappear.

Research examining the possible differences between clinical depressive and pervasive but nonclinical sadness states such as in bereavements has indicated a major variation in identity disturbances. High depression scores correlated to a significant degree with flattened identity experiences ($r = -.56$), whereas sadness scores did not (Kunzendorf, 2011). Morey et al. (2010) studied a large sample of people who were in and out of depressive states, over time, and found consistency in identity disturbances, in spite of fluctuation of levels of depression. Twenty-nine percent of patients with disturbed self–other attitudes were still depressed six years later, compared with only 6 percent of patients who were initially depressed and without comorbid disturbances in self–other attitudes. Such data indicates that self-states are not just halo effects from chemically imbalanced mood states, but that dysphoric personality style, or other personality disordered configurations, may combine in the causality of depressions. That is why Beck (1987) suggested that people who process new information with a bias toward negative self-beliefs had a proclivity for depression.

As depression heals or undergoes remission, the person might be able to counteract a negative attention bias by augmenting positive self-concepts. Self-identity theory may usefully address how and why negative and positive attentional bias toward information may shift self-schemas. It may also address the way in which each active self-schema influences how new information processing will be organized (Shestyuk & Deldin, 2010).

Stress and trauma disorders

Traumatic experiences may lead to dissociative identity disturbances or to states of depersonalization. Reality is perceived in a cloudy or even dream-like way, and remembered scenarios can seem more real than what is apprehended in the present moment. Posttraumatic stress disorder (PTSD) may follow. Identity disturbances in PTSD, adjustment disorders, and complicated grief include downgrading self-appraisals from competent to incompetent, attractive to unattractive, strong to weak, or harmonious to broken or fragmented. Blows to bodily integrity, such as having a myocardial infarction, stroke, amputations, or ostomy can lead to regressions into immature self-states. Similarly, major life events, such as being fired, going bankrupt, or being divorced, can have similar effects.

Until mastery over such stressor experiences creates a narrative process that can relate present to past identity, disturbances in conscious identity experience may persist. However, some people report identity growth to levels more mature and internally harmonious than those achieved even before the trauma or stressor events. Self-identity theory will need to explain the routes toward positive gains in self-definition, and the sense of enhanced identity coherence (Horowitz, 1990, 2012; Tedeschi & Calhoun, 1996).

Depersonalization

The conscious experience of depersonalization includes ongoing streams of awareness without a sense of self as agent. During the experience, the person may feel like an automaton, as described in this first-hand account:

> I think my thoughts are what start it. I start thinking about how fake I am and about how fake the world is. Then it hits me and I feel hollow. I feel like someone else is in control of my body, but at the same time I know it is really me. I can watch my arms typing this email to you, but it does not seem like they are my arms or my words. They belong to someone else. I also sometimes become aware of details of things and that makes it start too. At school last week, I was sitting in the library and started watching the other students. Soon they did not seem like real people. I could only see the colors of their clothes and hair, and the shape and size of the books they were reading. I looked down at myself and I seemed unreal, like a statue sitting there. Like my mind and my body were not even hooked together anymore and my mind was looking at this strange body that it did not belong in.
>
> (Joli, n.d., www.angelfire.com/home/bphoenixl/disspers.html)

Depersonalization is usually a momentary self-state, one that may return again and again. Some athletes are dedicated to performing well in a particular sport; they practice intently as they form an identity sense in adolescence. They can be devastated when an injury renders them incapable of continuing the self-reflecting physical activities. Episodes of depersonalization may occur until they re-schematize identity, so that additional self-attributes are valued. As mentioned for post-traumatic identity disturbance, such recoveries from depersonalization can help us develop a better theory of self-reorganizing schematizations in the neuroplastic brain, and teach us how to facilitate this growth.

Out-of-body experiences are related to reports of identity disturbance. The center of agency for the actions of the body is located in an imaginary self. This self is experienced quasi-perceptually, as is being in some other space. From this out-of-the-body vantage point, a constructed, conscious image of the actual body appears elsewhere and is controlled by the dislocated mind. People who have more visual imagery experiences are more likely to report such episodes (Parra, 2009). A comprehensive theory of the schemas of self can help explain such reconstructions of perception in the complex connectivities between the brain modules of information processing.

Dissociative identity disorder

Dissociative identity disorder is characterized by the existence of multiple, distinctive selves or personalities within the same individual (Kluft, 1984; Lowenstein, 1991; Kluft & Fine, 1993). These selves act, talk, and experience situations differently and may even have different handwriting. Alternative identities take control at the expense of a unified sense of self-definitions that are continuous over time. Memory of an alternate self-state may be seemingly unavailable to the currently active self-state. One patient describes the memory lapse:

> I "lost time," which is the symptom you read so much about, but I also had other symptoms like reading a letter an alter (alternative self) had written to people close to me, and not understanding it or remembering writing it. I was told all the time about conversations I had with other people that I did not remember.
>
> (Jolie, n.d., www.angelfire.com/home/bphoenix11disspers.html)

In addition to "losing time" when the alternate selves take over, a person may deny any knowledge of the alternates. In chaotic shifts of states, it may seem to observers as if incompatible, physically different people are in open conflict, competing to control the mind of one person.

Searles (1986) made the observation that suicidality often reflects one part of the mind wishing to "murder" another part of the mind. He said:

> A psychotherapist working with someone with dissociative identity disorder has the vital task of ascertaining which alter or ego state contains these murderous feelings and why. Often, such alters explain, once the therapist forms a "therapeutic alliance" with that alter, he or she may attempt to save the patient from some perceived danger. The alter of a patient I once saw in consultation told me she was so certain she was completely separate from the "person" (she used her legal first name) that she planned to stab the person in the abdomen, confident that she herself would not thereby be harmed. That is, she did not realize they shared the same body.
>
> (Searles, 1986, p. 85)

Different alters may appear in specific circumstances and can also differ in reported age and gender. McWilliams recounted a conversation with a patient's alter personality, which exemplifies how identities can be of differing and in open conflict:

> One evening I picked up my phone when my answering machine was beginning to record and found myself talking to a petulant child, an alter personality of a patient. She was calling to tell me about an early trauma whose existence I suspected, and to ask why the treatment-seeking part of the self needed to know about it. The next day when I told my client about the message, she asked to hear it. After listening, together, to my conversation with this dissociated aspect of herself, she was amused to note that she had not been feeling at all identified with the childish voice.
>
> (McWilliams, 2011, p. 344)

Self-identity theory needs to explain how various "selves" are kept as segregated configurations of associated meanings. How are these stored in memory and then activated into states of mind, with identity organized by attributes of the apparently alternative "selves?"

Prefrontal dementia

Prefrontal dementia may include a serious, enduring and progressively deteriorating lapse in the psychological ability to maintain a coherent sense of identity. The sense of *I*-ness itself may be lost in confusions between sources of information. Here is a case example found on the Internet and available to the public. The author notices memory losses and reduced, conscious, analytic capacities. Between the lines is a loss in the sense of self as having authority over actions:

> When a colleague came to me to get a copy of a computer program I had written a year or so before, I knew I was in big trouble. When I looked at the code I had written, I couldn't understand it.
>
> (http://bvftd.blogspot.com/p/mydiagnosis-dementia.html)

Conclusion

A theory needs to account for both failures to develop self-cohesion and a constant, reasonably accurate sense of identity, and also deterioration in what was once a stable, overall self-organization as a way of forming and interpreting conscious experiences. First, we will discuss psychological causes of identity problems and, then, the social contexts in which they occur (Chapters 3 and 4). We will consider the biological aspects of biopsychosocial interaction in causation of identity problems in Chapter 5, on neural connectivity factors.

In this chapter we have discussed some specific questions that our biopsychosocial integrative theory should answer. These questions deserve repetition, and I will summarize them at the beginning of Chapter 3.

Chapter 3

Learning self, psychologically

From such identity experiences and disturbances as noted in Chapter 2 we can derive questions that we would like to answer, as best we can, with a psychological theory that can mesh well with the social and neuroscience theories that we will address in the next two chapters. Here are the salient questions:

1   Some people exhibit lapses in accuracy of knowledge about themselves as related to others. How and why might they retain and repeat the same errors of self and other beliefs?
2   If some lapses in accurate self and other appraisals involve switching between binary extremes or incompatible beliefs, how and why are such views compartmentalized rather than associated?
3   Why is it difficult for some people to find their way to a continuous and coherent configuration that harmonizes, rather than segregates, their multiple self-concepts?
4   How is it that some disturbed persons have frequent irrational projections or introjections, confusing traits and intentions of self and other?
5   How might a person, aiming at avoiding entry into an intense and negatively emotional self-state—such as a potential for searing shame, for example— evoke irrational self-concepts such as grandiosity?

All of these questions ask how to conceptualize sub-portions of overall self-organization, and their degree or level of achieved coherence in a person. A cartoon in the *New Yorker* magazine depicted the difficulties in the path toward self-coherence. It showed two middle-aged persons, talking over coffee. One is saying to the other: "If only my identity were not so wrapped up in who I am!" It is our empathy for this shared, human predicament that causes us to chuckle. A solid, well-defined identity is a product of complex combinations of social reflectance, conscious emotional and conceptual thinking, and unconscious mental processes that activate various, unconsciously stored sets of information. Biological dispositions and social contexts will shape which meanings may be learned over the course of a lifetime. These meanings, their segregations or compartmentalizations in associational networks, and the degree of going beyond such dissociations of meaning will then determine which states of self may emerge, and which states of mind and variations in interpersonal behavioral patterns may manifest. Patterns of emerging self-states may improve as people redefine self, harmonize contradictions, and go beyond deficiencies in relationship capacities, so as to obtain better reflectance of their own identity. Learning to knit together discordant parts of self can improve a sense of continuity and coherence, but many of those discordant parts were found to be largely unconscious.

Conscious and unconscious information and mental processing

In a book called *The Discovery of the Unconscious*, Ellenberger (1970) reviewed what happened before and after Sigmund Freud, the symbolic father of such theory, found dreams to be "the royal road" to deep dramas producing strange-seeming views of self and relationships. As Ellenberger shows, Freud was not the first or last source of relevant observations and theory pertaining to the unconscious. Others, such as Charcot and Janet, also looked upon the unconscious as a container of "the repressed" aspects of self. Early studies assumed the amount of information involved in unconscious processes to be smaller than conscious sensation: thinking, feeling, and deciding what is realistic to do. Further investigation of mental activities showed that the extent of information being stored, appraised, and prepared for action preconsciously was actually much larger and more complex than initially supposed.

Freud started his theory with a model of mental topography, aiming to map "what was unconscious" and why. In 1920, Freud went beyond his topographic model of conscious, preconscious, and unconscious memories, dividing personality between three mental structures: the *id*, the *ego* and the *super-ego*. This was an attempt to define parts of self, though by ego he then meant the consciously identified self.

Freud followed Plato in seeing character as emerging out of instinctual drives he called the *id* (the "it" in German was translated into "id" for English literature). The *ego* was like the rider of a horse, a humanized self deciding where the powerful animal of drives and instincts would and would not go. The rider was also influenced by social upbringing. Part of the self internalized the morals of social values and was called the "over-I," the *superego*. Though a popularized model, the theory has since changed. Erikson (1959, 1968) especially found identity missing from classical psychoanalytic theory, and developed conceptualizations of key milestones of identity formation across the entire life cycle.

In addition to Erikson, many developmental psychologists, self-psychologists, and object-relations psychoanalytic theorists, writing from 1930 to the present, wrote that evolving self-organization occurs mentally as the person is socially embedded in, and learning from, the available caretakers. The self emerges within significant attachments. Each individual might have several sub-organized schemas of self, embedded in *role-relationship models*.

Klein (1957), Winnicott (1958), and Jacobson (1964) examined primitive, and even false, selves living in the unconscious mind in possibly quite segregated or even dissociated ways. Projective confusions—as to what characterized the self, and what characterized the other—occurred as roles were dislocated between self and other schematizations in role-relationship models (Kernberg, 1967; Kohut, 1971; Bion, 1997). Under this object-relations umbrella, Bowlby echoed the early Freud, of traumatic repressed memory fame, with his own emphasis on how childhood trauma and loss might leave a legacy of impaired identity and insecurity from anxious or bereft attachments. Subsequent research empirically proved aspects of the attachment theory (Srouf & Fleeson, 1986; Emde, 1988; Main & Solomon, 1990).

Contemporary models

From this quick summary of the background, we can turn to a modern theory to explain identity disturbances and answer the questions raised at the beginning of this chapter.

As in Chapter 1, we will use the term *person schema* to refer to an enduring and slowly changing psychological knowledge structure about the characteristics of self or another well-known person (called an object in psychoanalytic object-relations theories), when answering these questions. The characteristics of a person as generalized in a schema, which may function as a cognitive map of an individual, usually include traits, roles, fixed beliefs about the body, plans for ways of acting, ways for controlling emotionality, and intentions to follow certain desires, and fears of breaking certain rules, and core values. A schema functions as a kind of template for expectations, and as a script for potential action sequences, if an opportunity to release an intention should be perceived.

Schemas contain recorded experience. The mind/brain summarizes past information that might be used to chart future actions. The resulting patterns repeat behaviors over and over again. New schemas can develop as action and knowledge are modified to accord to new situations. Schemas provide a template for connecting information formed from different modules of memory, including implicit and explicit, declarative, and procedural knowledge (Piaget, 1962; Kihlstrom, 1987; Horowitz, 1991, 1998).

Multiple selves

Each person has a repertoire of self-schemas. Any one of the schemas can be activated to organize an appraisal of one's current role, as in a social interaction. Each self-schema operates as an associated network with established linkage strengths at the neural net level. Priming of its associational network is how activation of a particular schema occurs. Priming can occur at social, psychological, or neural levels of instigation, with interactive consequences affecting how priming continues.

An active schema influences a current state of mind; it operates to organize a current self-state. This may affect a current sense of identity and also may be down-influenced and down-regulated by a current sense of identity. Alternative, inactive self-schemas lie dormant, but other situations can re-activate them.

These self-schemas are a repertoire of meanings, stored unconsciously, potentially activatable. In unconscious information processing, a current set of perceptions, perhaps in a social situation, may be appraised, interpreted, reconfigured, and combined. Efforts at identity redefinition may affect these repertoires of self-schemas, the role-relationship models in which they nest, and their level of overall integration with each other.

The mental processes that are active can involve parallel streams of information affected somewhat differently by the active self-schemas and role-relationship models operative within that stream. In other words, a lot is going on unconsciously to appraise the meaning of what may be consciously perceived in the moment, or reviewed in memory or dreaming. To repeat: multiple self-schemas may be involved in parallel distributive processing of how to interpret what is going on, how to motivate and prepare for action, and whether or not to revise self-attributions and beliefs (Rummelhart & McClellan, 1986).

This parallel processing may occur before conscious trains of thought occur. Perhaps just one of the parallel streams may result in reflective awareness. The reason is that conscious trains of an emotional-cognitive nature are especially useful if attention is focused on problems that require logical analysis, choices in the midst of dilemmas, re-appraisals of what is happening, and prediction of what is really likely to happen next. The schemas contain information that may be of great predictive value but may also contain errors of habitual appraisal.

Consider a repertoire of self-schemas, held unconsciously, and periodically subject to selective activation. Suppose a particular self-schema is activated currently, and is serving as an important way of organizing many bits of information. This is the self-state, underlying a particular state of mind. If a different self-schema becomes activated, a shift in self-state can occur.

The subject may or may not be aware that the shift has taken place. The state of mind may be apparent to self, or not. Perhaps a shift in state of mind may be noted by others in a social interaction, and not noticed by internal conscious reflection. But, inner conscious reflection may take place and conceal aspects of an altered cognitive-emotional processing from others. That is, when there is a shift in activity of self-schemas the person can still, using reflective self-awareness, shape behavior, and so smooth out social patterns without displaying an explosive-seeming change in state of mind. This is an important aspect of emotional regulation.

Suppose that a usually optimistic person encounters a difficult setback and begins to doubt his or her own competence. Unconsciously, the setback can trigger a shift to a self-schema developed earlier, in situations where an important person treated him like a failure. This "memory" accounts for a shift in mental gears, the usually dormant incompetent self-schema takes hold. This change in self-state produces a change in state of mind from happy confidence to fear and self-doubt. Harmonizing aspects of the different self-schemas allows the person to know what is happening, and to modulate emotional expressions to others. Such smoothing and softening of the transitions between states allow the person to present a poised appearance though an inner change has occurred; but not every personality can contain the activation of alternative selves by self-reflection.

To recapitulate, theories of "transference templates" (Freud, 1910) and "object-relations units" (Klein, 1948; Winnicott, 1958; Jacobson, 1964; Kernberg, 1967) posit such unconscious repertoires of self-schemas. Self-schemas are often contained in role-relationship models, guiding social interactions, intentions, and expectations. As already discussed, role-relationship schemas are cognitive-emotional generalizations of how one might hope to reach wishful satisfaction and cope with feared threats, rejections, and narcissistic injuries. That is, self-schemas are contained within self–other models. The active model is what Bowlby and others refer to as inner working models, and these models are especially augmented for figures of significant attachment.

To repeat: Wishful motives might activate role-relationship models associated with previous episodes of success in gaining satisfaction, and aims for coping well with threats might activate more defensive, fear-avoiding role-relationship models.

Notoriously, an adult traumatic experience can activate a regression to a childhood trauma-related role-relationship model. A perceived betrayal or abandonment can activate weak and despairing schemas, strong and vengeful schemas, or even dissociative states of mind. One example consists of clinical syndromes that have been called complex PTSD (Herman, 1997; Horowitz, 2011).

Role-relationship models

Role-relationship models combine self-concepts with relationship concepts, containing expected action, response, and reaction patterns of interaction sequences. In the appraisal of a social situation, one role-relationship model from a repertoire might be the prime organizer of emotion, thinking, perceiving, and action planning; other role-relationship models might be involved in parallel, distributive, and unconscious information processing. Due to fundamental empathic abilities, the other may also be modeled as if the self, and felt as if the self, and this can lead to learning by identification and ready role-reversals.

Different emotions might be activated as the outcome of processing memory of an event by different role-relationship models. A friend might criticize my manuscript. One role-relationship model might be used in reappraising the memory of receiving that criticism: in it I feel confident in the positive nature of my reciprocity with this friend and as I review the critique I take his feedback as constructive, leading me to feel a medley of warmth, appreciation of the logic, and gratitude. Another role-relationship model might review the memory from a vulnerable self-schema, feel the critique as adding to self-doubt, leading me to feel embarrassed at asking for the reading and feedback in the first place. Both models potentially compete in unconscious processing to organize my conscious experiences of felt emotions on review of the memory.

Social situations: using different role-relationship schemas as possibly appropriate working models

The conscious mind may have a stream of conscious perceptions of what is happening in a social situation while at the same time, in parallel processing, the unconscious mind tries out many schemas in preconscious processing, seeking the best fit between inner templates and an emergent situation. Different self and other schemas organize appraisals in each line of information processing. In some kind of centralized workspace the mind's higher conceptual functions choose one, hopefully the best fit, for attention (Baars, 1986). That leads to the primary train of interpretive thought in a flow of conscious representations and reflective comparisons of primary perceptual streams and conscious reappraisals. Such high-level conscious reflection then leads to further checks for the accuracy of interpretations and, from there, to better and better problem solving. Decision-making and plan checking of possible actions can then occur at the highest level of conscious awareness.

Meanwhile, the mind continues to unconsciously search for the best fit of schemas to perceptions. It continues to inhibit or augment schemas until it finds the best choice. The appraisal of what works continues onwards in time during a here and now, self-and-other, transaction. Working models can be modified and expanded. Repeatedly valuable working models may then be recorded as enduring person schemas, such as better self-schemas in more adaptively appropriate role-relationship models.

New learning from new trials of how best to create optimum situations and better connect socially occurs, leading to improved maturity and wisdom.

With this base theory of how multiple schemas of persons operate in the mind, we can explain some but not all the shifts in self-state found in identity disturbances. If a person has multiple self-schemas, then they may shift within their repertoire, producing different self-states. But people vary, and such shifts are not experienced by most people as a disturbance in identity, rather just a shift in self-feeling and defining roles or values. All five questions asked at the beginning of this chapter required some kind of explanation in terms of levels of dissociation or connection within an individual's repertoire of person schemas. We need to consider levels of such connectivity if we want to understand more about why is it hard or impossible for some people to modify schemas in the direction of optimum adaptation and personality growth and how they may fail to integrate multiple self-concepts into a coherent and continuous self-organization so they can smooth out otherwise explosive transitions in self-states. We need to add a theory of unconscious and hierarchical organizational complexity of self-schemas and role-relationship models.

Overarching organizers

Supra-ordinate schemas are a kind of overarching organizer of a nest of subordinate self-schemas, acting like the chairman of a committee organizing its members.

In a metaphorical sense, each organized self-schema is a member of the committee, and the question is, how well does the chairman know what is going on within and between these committee members? In "the committee of selves," is there an agency in charge when choices and predictions are to be made? Some people have identity disturbances because they dissociate not only memories from different states, but knowledge of alternative selves. Supra-ordinate self-schemas that can contain and smooth out differences in self-schemas are inadequate to the task, at least in stressful conditions.

Several supra-ordinate schemas could be subsumed under overall self-organization that can function like the head of a department organizing many different committees. Supra-ordinate self-schemas can integrate the contradictions between a desired self-schema, a realistic, less-than-ideal self-schema, and a self-judging schema containing values used in criticizing the differences noted between ideal and real. Supra-ordinate self-schemas allow for self-reflection about subordinate beliefs and attitudes.

Without the smoothing-over effect of supra-ordinate schemas, a person might experience (and exhibit) a stark shift in identity with every shift in activity of the person schemas involved in current state of mind organization. For example, a parent might desire to experience a current moment of warmly nurturing a child, organizing a flow of conscious experience with a working model depicting the self as a loving mother, and the child as a cute, gratifying, and reciprocally loving toddler. Due to extreme exhaustion, the sensations of warm togetherness might not occur. The caretaking might feel too burdensome, and the parent, perhaps feeling eventually drained, may barely be able to maintain duties, experiencing the signals of the child as quite frustrating demands.

Without supra-ordinate integration, shifts between such role-relationship models, exacerbated by fatigue, can lead to explosive state changes, even to abuse. With a higher level of schemas, that is, with a supra-ordinate schema, the parent might feel a few resentful ideas toward a child's cries as micro-momentary thoughts, without expressing them, with full emotional modulation, and so without harshly condemning either the self or the child.

A supra-ordinate schema might be organized by self-definitions within a mother role, containing subordinate self-schemas such as strong mother, weak mother, cold mother, warm mother, and so on. A supra-ordinate schema might be organized by self-definitions as professor and chancellor of a large university, with subordinate self-schemas as excellent leader, imposter, embittered, empowered, and so on. The roles as mother, career woman, wife, daughter, political party guru, and so on might all have aggregate self-schemas, nested into associational complexity as supra-ordinate complex roles, and these nested hierarchically "upward" as overall self-organization. How well this nesting was integrated and harmonized would be levels of self–other schematic organization, an important clinical construct to be discussed in Chapter 6 and other chapters.

At a lower level of person schematic capacities, that is with deficits in supra-ordinate capacities, the parent just illustrated might feel like an all-good father (not to keep it in any gender) in one self-state, a self-righteous, child punisher in another self-state, and an all-bad, guilty, abusive father in another state. The important and commonly recognized clinical implication is that deficiencies in forming and maintaining the function of supra-ordinate schemas may impoverish the capacities for emotional regulation. Impulsive actions are more likely to occur, and that can lead to real remorse. To defend against guilt, blame can be shifted to the child. The hostility was due to the child "being bad." In this case, it would not readily be seen as abuse, but as a deserved, retaliatory punishment: "That will teach you."

We have discussed how a person who has developed supra-ordinate self-schemas will likely experience more continuity and sameness in his or her sense of identity, over time. Socially, the person will seem to smoothly shift roles, as from leader to follower, friend to supervisor, parent to offspring, creative to stagnant performer, intimate to adversary. At work, such a person can manage well the usual cooptition: that is the common blends of cooperation and competition with co-workers.

A person with self-reflective awareness of continuity in identity has enhanced self-acceptance and the ability to tolerate ambivalence. The more a person has harmonized conflicted elements into supra-ordinate person schemas, the more that person can accept contradictions and negative emotions. The person will be able to re-evaluate what is going on in situations such as moral dilemmas and strange new stressors.

Frustrations will be felt, but transitions between states of mind will be smooth rather than explosive. In sharp contrast, people who have not developed supra-ordinate schemas may exhibit impulsive behavior, perhaps compensating by using defenses that seriously distort reality; they excessively project bad traits away from self, onto the other who, then, is the one to blame (Vaillant, 2012).

People at lower levels of person schematic capacities may have limited ability to perceive, realistically appraise, and empathetically model the minds of others, in their own minds. If so, it is hard to for them to form apt schemas of other people, and good role-relationship models. They do build some person-in-relationship schemas, but the lack of accurate empathy that matches with perceptions of others creates a sense of doubt about relating. Impairments in this range of capacities mean that new information is not processed well.

When negative emotions are felt, the location may even be unclear. Is the self hostile or under attack from a predatory but perhaps deceitfully "nice" other? The impoverished capacities for apt information processing in the mind can lead to suspicion, remoteness, expression of bizarre behaviors or aversion to the usual non-verbal and verbal aspects of social communication. As a further consequence, impoverished social interactions lead to a lack of reflections of self, and so perhaps to disturbed identity experiences.

Figure 3.1 graphically depicts the hierarchical assembly of self-organization, from subordinate to supra-ordinate structures of schematized meanings. Table 3.1 summarizes the person schemas theory just presented, boiled down into ten principles.

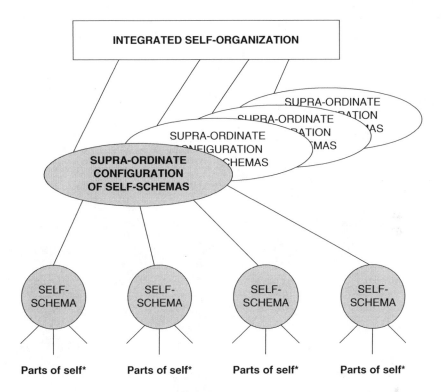

Figure 3.1 Integrated self-organization

Table 3.1 Principles of self-organization

1	Schemas are organized knowledge structures that can fill in or delete information, in order to speed information processing and integrate output from various modules of the brain.
2	Schemas are both maintained and changed unconsciously through, and in the context of, trials of perception and action, making predictions and appraising consequences.
3	Person schemas are cognitive maps pertaining to self, others, and role-relationship transactional models.
4	Multiple self-schemas exist in the repertoire of a person and may have contradictory patterns.
5	The activity levels of self-schemas vary, producing different conscious experiences and behaviors as recurrent states.

(Continued)

Table 3.1 (Continued)

 6   Control processes may alter the activity levels of schemas to avoid emotional turmoil, potential self-disorganization, and dreaded states.
 7   Self-schemas exist in nested hierarchies as more complex linkages of associational networks develop.
 8   People with more supra-ordinate self-schemas can experience more coherence and continuity in their sense of identity.
 9   Antithetical elements between self-schemas make it more difficult to develop supra-ordinate schemas.
10   Defensive distortions—to prevent intense negative emotions—do reduce the threat of dreaded states, but, when habitually used, limit coherence in overall self-organization.

The developing self

As suggested in Table 3.2, the first stage of identity development is categorical separation of what is self and what is other. Following Erikson's model of the life cycle as a sequence of social and developmental dilemmas, even at this early stage there may be adaptive or potentially maladaptive (but not irreversible) outcomes. This distinction between self and other, in terms of manifest behaviors, seems to occur by two months of age (Stern, 1985).

The next stage occurs between two and six months of age. The baby gains the sense of being an entity that controls a body. This sense of agency relates to some primitive recognition of the caregiver as a separate agency, responding to or withholding from the baby. Between seven and nine months, the infant seems to develop a much more subjective sense of self, and to know the possibility of other states of mind. A new ability emerges. The infant can tune in to the mental states of others through learning the meanings and emotional colorations of vocal tone, facial expressions, and bodily movement. This combination of early individuation and empathy for another is probably the onset of healthy narcissism and learned love, adding to instinctive identification and attachment behaviors (Lewis, Amini, & Lannon, 2000).

Between 15 and 18 months the child is also developing a storehouse of information about what parental figures believe is good and bad. The child learns effective and ineffective, doable and not doable role-relationship models, and is learning to manipulate this knowledge internally in order to decide how to act in different social situations. Now there can be a sense of self-constancy, of continuity of an "I" over time (Sandler & Rosenblatt, 1962; Lichtenberg, 1975).

The less secure the sense of connection to vital others, the more fragile this fledgling sense of self may become. An enfeebled sense of self may exist if resonance from parental figures is limited. A fearful, depressed, or preoccupied parent may give only meager empathetic feedback, increasing a sense of anxiety over attachment security in the child (Mahler, 1968; Bowlby, 1969; Stolorow & Lachmann, 1980; Lichtenberg, 1983).

Table 3.2 Self-development summarized

Period	Development of identity traits
1 Infancy	Accomplishment: first beliefs about the self as a separate entity. Deficit: fragments of sensation not organized as of the self.
2 Early childhood	Accomplishment: sense of competence of self and beliefs about various, possible, future roles. Deficit: insufficient agency as a self with initiative.
3 Middle childhood	Accomplishment: multiple self-schemas with flexible shifts between them. Deficit: rigidity or chronically self-doubting and fearful.
4 Early adolescence	Accomplishment: resilient use of multiple self-schemas and formation of some supra-ordinate self-schemas. Deficit: identity diffusion.
5 Late adolescence	Accomplishment: supra-ordinate self-schemas. Deficit: propensity for dissociations.
6 Young adulthood	Accomplishment: harmonious configurations in sense of identity. Deficit: identity disturbances.
7 Middle adulthood	Accomplishment: stable hierarchy of personal values. Deficit: self-disgust.
8 Older adulthood	Accomplishment: narrative sense of identity as having continuity over decades. Deficit: bitterness or lapses in self-esteem.

Investigators found that early attachment styles can persist as adult role-relationship models. These include securely attached, insecurely attached, ambivalent, and relationship-resistant (Ainsworth, 1973; Main, 1975; Ainsworth et al., 1978; Bretherton & Waters, 1985; Sroufe & Fleeson, 1986; Emde, 1988; Main, Hesse, & Kaplan, 2005). The securely attached person can tolerate more stress. The anxiously attached person has less self-confidence. The ambivalently attached person seems to expect harm or rejection, and so is more likely than others to exhibit detachment or variability in love and hate. A dismissively attached person will emotionally distance self from others.

Adult identity in the context of role-relationship schematizations

Marriages provide good examples. A spouse may experience the relationship as a "we," with mutual facilitation and sharing of warm states of kindness, caring, tenderness, and sympathy. At other times, he or she experiences anger, frustration, and pining for "something that is missing in the relationship." The negative states are only mildly distressing if there is implicit recognition of the positive states which are likely to be restored. Trust is built into a supra-ordinate role-relationship model. On the other hand, a self-schema of being a spouse harmed by neglect leads to a different, much more distressing emotionality, if it is not contained in an over-all positive supra-ordinate schematization.

A person with a low level of self and other schematization can split relationship states into all good and all bad models. In frustration, or when upset by surges of anger from within, the self-state activated may be one of being a victim under attack by a predator. Emergence of such hostile role-relationship models, with-out the moderation of supra-ordinate schemas, leads to a self-fulfilling prophecy. Fearing attack or loss, the person damages and ends a relationship, leading to real loneliness and despair.

Imitation and identification

Children naturally see caregivers, usually parents, as extensions of protean views of self. They imitate facial expressions and try to duplicate actions. Seeing that the child is trying to imitate her, the parent says, "Not this way," imitating how the child has done something, and then says, "But this way," showing how to do it in a more desirable way. In the process, the child learns what kind of imitation elicits positive and negative responses from the parent.

Parental figures teach the rules. And, after all, because of their power, parents may seem as if they are "always right." If something goes wrong in a family, a divorce, for example, or an episode of depression, sometimes the child blames him or herself. If empathic parents do not clarify reality appropriately, the child may grow with an enduring tendency toward criticizing the self first, "I am the problem."

When a child falls and cries, a parent soothes the child and applies a band-aid to the abrasion, teaching how to care for a minor injury to the knee. The child may put a band-aid on a doll or pet. The child learns how to care for things. In such ways, a developing child uses parental example to construct their own roles and sense of future identity.

Suppose, for example, a child has a parent who giggles nervously when some-one else speaks in an angry tone of voice. The child may watch and hear the parent and mimic the response of giggling and, with many repetitions, will acquire this as a habit. Even though unaware of the habit, the child may, when anger is in the air, giggle nervously. As a sum total of many such episodes, a child may identify with timidity. Identification may involve not only this bit-by-bit assembly by observa-tion and mimicry, but also the development of a holistic schema of another person. The child may, then, adopt aspects of this schema as a self-view. Identification assimilates aspects of another person into the self. It preserves a continuity of roles across generations.

Trauma, abuse, and neglect

The child is not only separate but also, compared to the parents, smaller and more vulnerable. A child is easy to abuse, torment, ignore, or exploit. Contained by care, these proto-identities are dependent, not bad. And parents usually teach aptly about implicit growth: "You are so big! So strong! So capable!" They smile and their eyes gleam. The child learns, "I am good!"

Even good parents may be unable to shield a child or themselves in situations where domestic violence occurs. A child may develop an excessively helpless self-schema through identification with a helpless parent. Without adequate protection, a child may be vulnerable to use only fragmentary sub-self-schemas. The result may be the kind of identity disturbances that include feelings of falling apart or having bodily emptiness (Winnicott, 1958; Stolorow & Lachmann, 1980; Alvarez, 2010).

Trauma can lead to a sense of unreality and depersonalization. Some experiences are so unbearably painful that the child mentally "checks out." He or she may experience a stream of raw sensations that are not digested into self-identification. The self is, in effect, removed from the turmoil by numbing. A potential, lasting effect of trauma is habitual dissociation of person schematic beliefs and so to lapses in narratives, splitting of memories, and lowered regulation of social and self-conscious emotions.

Such dissociation can lead to the alternating self-states noted in the dissociative identity disorders and some borderline personality disorders, as described in Chapter 2. The splitting of self-schemas can also lead to compartmentalization of true and false selves (Winnicott, 1958) or dissociation of good and bad memories (Klein, 1948; Fairbairn, 1954; Kernberg 1967, 1976, 1992; Marmar & Horowitz, 1986; Horowitz, 1998). Only one set of memories is available to conscious experience at a time, and the set is as if forgotten in other self-states. Early dissociation, not ameliorated by developmental effects, can lead to trouble at every phase of the life cycle dilemmas as described by Erikson (1970), as simplified in Table 3.2, leading to disintegration rather than integration of identity, or maintenance of a defensively negative identity to avoid diffusion and chaos of inner sensation of self.

Internalization and externalization

Some observations of identity disturbances that require theoretical explanation concern irrational shifts of attribution, mixing the attributes of self up with traits of others, and vice versa. Faced with vulnerability to being harmed in a turbulent, unpredictable, and threatening situation, a child may focus on the most powerful figures in the immediate environment. If these people are aggressors and the child is a victim, the child may prefer to reverse roles and *identify with the aggressors* because, being strong, they have the best survival potential. Having identified the self with aggressors, the child, when older, may assume an identity of aggressor and victimize others to avoid the victim role for themselves. We call this kind of identity-schema formation a *role reversal.*

A fluid process of internalization and externalization is involved in a mental operation called *projective identification* (Klein, 1948; Masterson, 1980; Grotstein, 1981; Kernberg, 1982). In projective identification, an aspect of the self is removed from the self-schema and placed, instead, in the working model, as the role and attribute of another person. A meaningful person, such as a relative, lover, or boss, gets the blame for hostility, for example. In projective identification, the subject remains close to the person in whom the bad trait is felt to be located, but the closeness is often marked by hostility toward the other for having the bad trait. By behaving aggressively, the subject may indeed provoke the other into wishing to hurt or abandon the subject. This hostility within the other is now "there."

Idealization and self-esteem

A child sometimes learns irrational degrees of idealization of another to protect against their own sense of deflation. Excessive idealization of some figure in the child's world may bring frustration and deflation when that figure does not fulfill the child's expectations. Hope in the idealized figure may turn to rage, as the child blames the supposedly caring and trustworthy person for betrayal (Kernberg, 1976).

Since idealization of the self may also be used to protect against deflated and weak self-concepts, the child may develop unusually grandiose self-schemas. These may be associated with ambitions for greatness. Such ambitions may also be fostered by identification with fictional heroes. If the child is talented, the real skills developed from this context may lead to continued adult expectations of great recognition for great achievements. When the world does not provide realization of such high hopes, and if the person cannot accept real limits, chronic and bitter traits of character may result, along with a lapse in self-esteem.

Conclusion

The task of an early phase of psychological self-identity formation is the generation of a series of self-concepts in the context of social relationships. These beliefs about the roles and definitions of self become organized and generalized into self-schemas. Self-schemas may be configured together into supra-ordinate self-schemas, lending progressively more coherence in personality functioning over time.

Chapter 4

Social learning and identity formation

Social interactions shape individual identity formation and self-organizational maintenance. The intra-psychic schemas of self and other contain the precipitants and generalizations of the interactions. The most important social residues are role-relationship models since these models organize traits of self in affiliation with attributes of others in networks that include transactional scenarios or scripts, values, and potentialities for emotional expressions.

The transmission of meanings in cultures is not necessarily clear in the sense of verbal descriptors. The residues of the meanings from cultures, within a person, are not necessarily conscious. The important issue is that both levels, social and intra-psychic, are often implicit rather than explicit, procedural and enacted rather than declarative in the form of verbal statements. Exploring the social derivations of identity qualities is one aspect of that famous Freudian phrase, making the unconscious conscious.

Where Freud emphasized instinctive biological drives such as the libido and aggression, Erik Erikson emphasized self-development within social structures, starting with extreme dependency on caretakers. He developed important models of how to examine identity formation in social contexts in this early phase and connected them to subsequent development in a model of the human life cycle. He summarized the key acquisitions of identity features in a slowly maturing self, operating for survival within a culture, a culture that existed before birth, and a culture that itself might be changing (Erikson, 1950, 1959, 1968; Bion, 1997; Erikson & Erikson, 1998).

A contemporary model of the sequential development of self was summarized in Chapter 3, in Table 3.2. That table summarized how simpler schemas formed into more complex units (Piaget, 1962; Piaget & Inhelder, 1969). Values are an important aspect of this progressive developmental articulation of individuals to communities. Values are used to appraise the worth of a person in society, affecting the roles the individual might select for skill development and eventual self-esteem. The person learns about appraising self as if from the value perspectives of others as well as self-owned and personally prioritized values.

The same periods of self-development used in Table 3.2 are repeated in Table 4.1. Two columns add the key tasks for the developing person to accomplish during each part of life, and the positive versus negative social outcomes that may result. An initial source of conflict in social values is inherent where, due to many changes in society, it is unlikely that all the attitudes of the mother and father will be identical, and children are raised by a variety of parental figures. As the individual ages, social influences and especially peers will add further to psychological value conflicts, many of which will operate unconsciously.

As psychoanalysts know, each parent is likely to have his or her own personal self-organizational conflicts to pass on to the next generation. The optimum personal identity of the maturing person who was their child requires that he

Table 4.1 Community and self-development

Period	Personal and social tasks	Identity and relationship schemas
1 Infancy	Attain secure attachments to other people. Elicit affection and nurturance. Social expectations are that dependency needs will be met by society if parents fail.	Positive outcome: secure role relationship models. Negative outcome: angry detachment, or insecure role relationship models.
2 Early childhood	Increase bodily control. Develop sense of right and wrong. Learn communication skills and to negotiate. Connect gender beliefs to social roles.	Positive outcome: beliefs that lead to confidence and empathy for others. Negative outcome: self-preoccupation and socially anxious role relationship models.
3 Middle childhood	Experiment with gender characteristics. Relate to peers. Form close friendships. Learn to work on one's own. Enlarge sense of morality by sharing rules with peers.	Positive outcomes: self-restraint in relation to the rules of social contexts. Negative outcomes: impulsive selfishness.
4 Early adolescence	Accept one's changing body. Explore sexuality. Forge trust in peer groups. Develop work and recreational abilities.	Positive outcome: apt core values. Negative outcome: excessive conformity or authoritarianism.
5 Late adolescence	Improve regulation of emotion. Extend understanding of gender and sexual roles. Develop specific work skills.	Positive outcome: core values that balance cooperation, competition, and independence. Negative outcome: inconstancy of responsibility, duty, and commitments.
6 Young adulthood	Relate self to social systems for work, new families, and groups. Learn about friends who may also harm or be inconstant rather than reliable.	Positive outcome: responsibility for duties. Negative outcome: excesses or paralysis of participation in groups.

7	Middle adulthood	Accept illness and loss without giving up. Care for older generation, lead younger generation.	Positive outcome: schemas for leadership and appropriate use of power. Negative outcome: excesses or paralysis in social power use.
8	Late adulthood	Accept aged body. Adapt to retirement. Confront transience. Pass on leadership. Transmit core values to younger generations.	Positive outcome: satisfaction in faith that values will survive personal death. Negative outcome: sense of failure and loss of self-coherence when loses power to control others.

or she forge some kind of harmonization of alternative forms, just as changing societies have to both maintain and alter their traditions. While many value conflicts operate unconsciously, values are particularly apt for verbal representation, becoming conscious, and communicable in clear lexical statements. That is the reason why values and value conflicts are one important way to examine identity definitions both within the mind and in social settings (Gatersleben, Murtagh, & Abrahamse, 2012).

Infancy and childhood

As discussed in Chapter 3, the depositions of social life seem to occur quite early, when infants develop a secure and trusting sense of affiliation with an adequate parenting figure. This positive outcome of social interactions is what Bowlby (1969, 1973) called *secure attachment*. Erikson called this kind of affiliation the establishment of *basic trust* and in psychohistories he showed how this social to intra-psychic progression promoted later personality traits of vitality versus apathy, and optimism versus pessimism.

A more negative outcome in the establishment of basic role-relationship models may occur if and when parenting or caretaking figures are inimical, inconsistent or neglectful, or when communities suffer tragedies, warfare, or economic collapse. A child may develop a negative internal model of the "other" as a threat or enemy. Such negative personality traits as suspicion, anger, detachment, and despair may develop and persist if not later tempered by later advances and modifications of core schemas. Adolescence is a time when such modification seems especially possible, otherwise traits such as negative biases in earlier attachment-based expectations of others may endure through adulthood and even be passed on to the next generation (Klein, 1948; Ainsworth, 1973; Main, 1975; Sroufe, 1979; Kagan, 1982; Bretherton, 1985; Sperling & Berman, 1991).

Adolescent development

As the child becomes an adolescent and moves beyond the family, new experiences lead to a reevaluation of childhood beliefs related to self-definition. One developmental task of adolescence is to forge a peer group and use that as a new point of view from which to reflect back on self-definitions as related to others. Existing relationship schemas are broadened. New role-relationship models evolve, often based on bodily changes with connected sexual and social experimentations. Trials of new friendships, first attempts at romantic relationships, alliances, and betrayal of alliances usually take place (Blos, 1979; Brody, Moore, & Glei, 1994).

While experimenting with various possibilities for social status, many adolescents attach themselves to social groups by sharing values. Shared values, rituals, and rules supplement the pragmatics of survival through affiliation. The group membership shapes selfhood and forms symbols by which to claim or stake out an identity for others to witness.

Following the rules of shared values within the peer group becomes very important, for defiance or innovation also define identity. Being ostracized by a social group is often extremely painful for an adolescent, and sacrifices are made to obtain and keep one's standing with peers. The sub-groups set their own symbols, norms and rules, sometimes running counter to those of larger society. For instance, in many American cities, teenagers consider high school acts of delinquency such as smoking, drinking alcohol, taking street drugs, truancy, or defying authority as socially desirable and "cool."

The prerequisites of social status and the perils of transgression are drawn into self-defining cognitive maps. Character begins to solidify as plans develop for handling expected challenges and dilemmas. For instance, the adolescent may conform to a peer group excessively; become a person who strives always to be in control of others; or, feeling stigmatized, or different, chooses an eccentric and solitary path. The self-definitions may be plural and not harmonized, leading to fluctuations between alternative self-states that are now more prominent in comparison with how far other adolescents have developed in personality consistency.

In this structure of meaning-of-self as established in peer groups, the late adolescent begins to weave a broader tapestry of future plans. Sustained commitments can be established. Love is explored as a mutual relationship, possibly resulting in a long-term commitment, and relationships are explored for group affiliations. Work roles are examined, commitments are revised, and social status is gained or lost. The results precipitate as enduring attitudes that may not be readily available to verbal representations, conscious reflection, and communication.

Adulthood

By adulthood, the individual may arrive at values for enlightened self-interest and commitments to others that represent a balancing point between freedom and responsibility. The adult lives in a variety of balancing acts between conflicting values. All the values may seem intuitively "good" but some are better than others, and choices between contradictory ones must be made. These choices, some socially forced, also define identity, and how it is or is not reflected back by perceptions and appraisals of messages from potential community or familial supports and sources of threat.

As skills, powers, and possessions are accrued, the possibility for the corruption of character increases. By corruption, I mean excessively self-centered governance of actions, without internalized moral restraints. The individual may exhibit a readiness to abandon goals and rules in order to gain wealth and short-term pleasures, or victory over others. Entitlement as a character trait may occur.

Responsibility for self and others is practiced as the alternative to either ruthless self-aggrandizement or self-impairing abnegations. The balance between work, intimacy, and socialization is explored during the adult stage of development. Spirituality, perhaps beyond the faith inculcated in childhood, is explored. A sense of belonging is lost, regained, strengthened or weakened, all with effects on identity.

By middle age, some people have gained control by becoming responsible caretakers and having jobs with authority and power while others may have been disappointed when ambitions, hopes, and cherished goals were not reached. A discrepancy between the values internally defined as an ought-to-be self, and an actual as self-appraised set of social connections can lead to an alteration between shame and bitterness that will be explored more fully in Chapter 8.

As the body declines in old age, even people with well-developed identity face the time to relinquish their power, control, and leadership. They can, however, develop a legacy of good deeds and a faith that their values will persist after their death. This sense of leaving some good for others can lead to a sense of continuing integrity of self-organization (Jung, 1934–1954; Erikson, 1959, 1968).

Life is a course in identity development. As a person develops, they create schemas, but may have difficulty harmonizing them within supra-ordinate configurations. Life development research suggests that normal people may not feel an inner sense of solidity, continuity, and coherence in identity until into their fifth decade of living, even in communities of rich opportunity (Levinson, 1996).

The balancing act between freedom and responsibility

In the balancing act between freedom and responsibility, each individual imagines how others, in the present moment, regard him. He is motivated to gain respect and avoid embarrassment. He does not want to be harmed, shamed, neglected or abandoned. To stabilize identity, an individual is strongly motivated to find shared values, and may even become motivated to die for them. For example, concepts of duty are social aspects of shared core values; acting on these concepts as in dying for one's country or religious group allows the individual to gain respect and so self-esteem.

A person can be put in this type of moral dilemma. To a soldier, a family at home may mean that he should stay behind in combat, to be there for his family rather than taking risks. His comrades expect him to show courage and leadership, to go forward and take risks. His value priorities dictate which self-schema may be activated to control actions in the moment: he is a father caring for young children and a wife, he is a soldier bonded to his team and aimed at the enemy as defined by his country. Balancing means harmonizing these roles with supra-ordinate value structures: this balancing or shifting abruptly between self-states takes place largely unconsciously.

An important aspect of identity as an American means having learned to internalize and commit to shared democratic values including liberty, justice, and equal rights. In the course of development, if one does not find these values to be shared, forming such an identity as an American becomes more conflictual. Such conflicts tended to occur more in the past than now if one was non-white, if one was female, or illiterate, because such citizens were denied votes, and that fact of life contributed to the devaluation of the person because of the negative social reflectance. This devaluation led toward self-stigmatization. The social devaluations also brought shame upon the American identity.

Various American sub-cultures currently continue this debate about affirmative action in acceptance into higher education, whether women are to be considered equal to men in getting comparable salaries for the same job, or whether heterosexuality is the exclusive way to legally marry. These controversies deeply impact identity and self-esteem just as slavery left a legacy of harm to, and social stigmatization of, the African-American identity. Long after slavery ended, the stigma of belonging to the enslaved group remained and was counteracted by shared values of pride, symbolized and ritualized in practices that reflected positively upon individual members. Developing identity coherence in spite of such "hurt" could make an emerging group member stronger in character, wiser, and more resilient than someone who has never been called upon to experience and overcome that same type of adversity. Community messages about the worth of any given group can enhance as well as undermine both social roles and self-appraisals from a socially reflected point of view.

Unconscious values and explicit declarations of self-defining values

Values are often unconscious. Indeed, putting values into words is often a hard task even in the intensive concentration and reciprocal verbal conversations of a psychoanalytic treatment (Horowitz, 2009). Making specific semantic statements of self–society values helps to clarify conflicts that can disrupt the goal of developing the harmonizing and supra-ordinate self-schematizations discussed in Chapter 3, and, in terms of disturbed levels of personality functioning, discussed in Chapter 6. Addressing this issue, Bronfenbrenner (1979) suggested that an individual develops values by living within five surrounding social contexts, with the individual in the center.

In the *microsystem*, the first layer, one finds closest relationships, such as those between parent and child, as well as sibling relationships. Consider Jenny, an 8-year-old girl growing up in Los Angeles in the 1990s. Jenny's microsystem included her single divorced mother, siblings, teachers, and friends. Her sibling order as oldest dictated the value of seniority. Her uncle's scorn for her mother suggested male gender was more powerful than seniority. The values of one teacher that it was wrong to wear shorts to school conflicted with the values of her friends that it was best to feel as cool as possible on hot days, and that some rebellion against standards was good because it showed a valued autonomy. Jenny could feel unsupported in a particular self-state, within this microsystem, if she was reflected by others close to her who did not share her values.

The second layer, the *mesosystem*, describes an *interaction between microsystems* surrounding Jenny, as in interactions between her environments at school and at home. When at age 13 Jenny got average grades at school, her ambitious mother met with Jenny's teachers who felt that average was not alright. The outcome was that teachers agreed that Jenny ought to function way above the average of her peers. Mother and teacher sent a joint message to Jenny that she needed to study more to attain everyone's approval. Jenny built a motto that functioned intuitively in her self-appraisals: that work is more important than play.

So Jenny amplified and formed her internal self-critic to foster more hours of study. But in her religious community, which met twice a week, Jenny was supposed to read the Bible more than her schoolbooks. Spiritual growth values conflicted with academic excellence values. Jenny recognized such conflicts, but it was hard to make it that clear in her thoughts. She studied both even harder, and playing with friends suffered reduced time. While securely attached to her mother, she did not develop best friends.

The third layer, the *exosystem*, illustrates the interaction between the microsystem with other environmental factors. Take, for example, Jenny's mother's workplace, which suffered as an institution when demand for its products fell with an economic slump. When Jenny's mother's supervisor fired some workers and raised work performance standards for those who remained, like Jenny's mother, Jenny's mother stayed at work longer hours and became more withdrawn and frustrated at home. Jenny, too young to understand that she had nothing to do with her mother's change, tried to please her mother and restore her approving reflectance by trying even harder in school. She also identified with her mother's tendency to blame others for her frustrations. She spent long hours over work in her room, socially isolated, and not getting optimum adolescent reflectance of alternative identity possibilities.

The fourth layer is the *macrosystem*. This system includes the influence of religion, culture, and economy on Jenny. Computer advances exploded into new economic possibilities, just as local cultures splintered and religious attendance waned. Jenny's family belonged to a church that informed her that important values were to work hard, help others, avoid harmful actions, and be a social joiner. Meanwhile, her suburban environment and surrounding media extolled values of competition, being a winner, and staying ahead of competitive peers at all costs. Jenny avidly studied computer programming in all her spare time, it seemed a way to excel and it did not suffer from her being clumsy in social interactions.

The fifth and largest layer is the *cronosystem,* representing both the passage of time and the passage of historical time periods. Jenny had many more options, opportunities, and different expectations as a young woman growing up late in the twentieth century now than she would have had growing up even 25 years earlier, as her mother had. She was now expected to have a career with prestige and make more money than her mother. The changing times allowed Jenny to use the Internet to form a business. Breaking away from the expected path to collegiate education, the company she invented made a substantial amount of money using unexpected, bold, and creative products; this boosted Jenny's self- and social esteem. She became a late bloomer in the dating world, developing late some concepts of herself as a sexual person.

Jenny favored her own choices over socially conventional ones of staying in college and going for post-graduate professional education. Her relative social isolation made romance a virtually non-existent value until she felt, later than her peers, "what can be next?" A combination of the historical changes in social expectations and social rewards, opportunities, and technological advances, made a path viable for Jenny that was not available for Jenny's mother, but also meant the path to parenthood was unclear. There were potential value conflicts within Jenny: high financial success and the time it took, versus concepts of a good life balancing professional values and values or roles for becoming a spouse and mother. For Jenny, it was multiple potential roles, developed at her different chronological milestones, within a society changing its chronologically determined values, and within other family and other societies extolling more traditional values.

Identity formation within the balancing act between self-oriented and other-oriented core values

Research shows that some people habitually favor self-serving choices and some people habitually favor group-oriented choices (Blatt & Luyten, 2009). Similarly, some cultures like Northern Europe or the USA promote individuality, while other cultures may embrace a collectivist mindset, one in which group values are given higher priority than values that favor individuality and individuation.

In suburban North America, being independent is something that is culturally valued in some sectors of the socio-economic spectrum. Children are expected to become self-sufficient by their early twenties and move out of their parents' homes around age 18. The pursuit of wealth, success, and individual self-expression is currently emphasized in the upper middle classes. On the other hand, other cultures favor interdependence, belonging to a group, and remaining a deeply embedded member of a community. Excessive independence in those cultures is not seen as positive, and may be seen instead as a trait representing greed or vanity.

Most people work in a context where they seek to gain respect and allegiance from individuals both above and below: they accept supervision and they teach others. In US culture, if people pay too much attention to their domestic and recreational lives, they may lose favor at work. In some locales, particularly in urban centers, the ratio of identity has shifted from family to a more remote and time-consuming work in an economic community. All this social reflectance affects self-esteem, self-coherence, and self-continuity or maintenance.

Placing greater emphasis on work-related identity has influenced the way we see ourselves and others, as noted in the imposter syndrome, in Chapter 2 on identity disturbances. This cultural emphasis of identity derived from work has led many people to base more of their self-esteem on work, which creates obvious problems upon retirement. When an individual retires, his conscious sense of self—his time structure, perceived role reflected by others, and his sense of purpose—is reduced (Barnes & Parry, 2004). Ingrained attitudes such as "a man is as good as his work productivity" lead to critical self-judgments when work is not available, especially after long habituations to its practices. So these out-of-awareness values, in the background, can powerfully affect mood and influence expectations of impending shame or glory (Goffman, 1961; Overall & Gorham 1962; Lewis, 1971; Kohut, 1972).

The balancing act: gender, sexual orientation and community attitudes

Feminism led to the modification of traditional gender role attitudes in many communities. Most women (at least in the middle and upper classes of the United States, in the beginning of the 19th Century) were expected to stay home to raise a family and take care of the household. Their participation in the workforce was very limited. Some stereotypes and beliefs about women that are today considered negative, in the same demographic, were then considered the norm. Most women today are expected to work outside the home, and those not working may be socially stigmatized. In urban centers, developing a career from 20–30 years of age may be given a higher priority than marrying and becoming a mother.

Similarly, many men no longer feel compelled to conform to a rigid mold as sole provider for the family: they can explore other roles, including being the primary child care provider. Young people today may face immense pressures, expecting themselves to be successful financial providers, great at their careers, and superior as mothers and fathers (Slaughter, 2012). In the past, clear transmissions of tradition across generations stabilized roles and identity. Now, the increase in acceptable, potential roles and self-defining identities leads to more routes and available options, as well as potentially more uncertainty.

Sexuality is a key factor in the articulation of the autonomous individual to evolved societies. *Queer theory* (Butler, 1990) led to a new approach to discussing the traditional values about gender, sexuality, freedom, and responsibility. These discussions have led to actions, as in current social changes of laws. Changes affecting identity are quite active in the individual–society transmission of values for understanding gay, lesbian, transgender, and other identities previously regarded as eccentric.

Social stigmatization and a lack of tangible support from the larger community may undermine a secure sense of identity. Studies of gay and lesbian youths (Rotheram-Borus & Langabeer, 2001), in the development phase of their sexual orientation, suggest that the following process occurs as a generalization with many individual exceptions: First, gay and lesbian youths begin a phase of discovery that sexual attraction is toward the same gender. This initial stage often manifests as a diffuse sense of belonging to gay or lesbian groups when sexual preferences begin to express themselves with recognition of what stimuli lead to erotic responses. With experiences and choices, a sexual component to identity is established. After this awareness stage, the person may progressively form new self-definitions, and experience some aspects of a shared identity across generations and in societies (Kroger, 2007). These stages go on through later aspects of ife. The end stage is an integration of one's self-recognized sexual orientation as harmonized with other parts of self-schematization, including gender and age, as accompanied by a passage to a social expression, and schematization of roles in communities.

Modern societies are becoming more accepting of alternative life styles: lesbian, gay, transgender, and bisexual included. But in the past, non-heterosexual aspects of identity were forbidden in some cultures and therefore stigmatized. Of course, some cultures also forbade some heterosexual aspects of behavior or even thought, as well as some modes of expressing gender.

As an example of identity strain in cultural milieux, over a quarter of gay men in a California research study reported they had been victims of violence or property damage because of their gay identity (Herek, 2009). On the other hand, attempts at "passing" for heterosexual, as an adaptive protection strategy, was reported by that segment of reporting subjects as damaging to their inward and conscious sense of self-definition and cohesiveness of parts of self. Stigmatization is a problem whenever personal identity is challenged by some groups of society.

Stigmatization of psychiatric disorders

General issues of stigmatization of mental disorders and developmental differences affect what a person thinks of him or herself, because identity is embedded in the reflectance of self and role as messages, verbal and non-verbal, are received from others. Concepts of what is normal in psychology and psychiatry have broadened considerably from earlier views (Rotheram-Borus & Langabeer, 2001) but social stigmatization can still lead to self-stigmatization. Self-critics can condemn parts of self for mental capacities, interactive styles, gender, or sexual preference, and this can promote inner dissociation of self-states rather than harmonization of overall self-organization.

Helping people be safe, containing reflectance of their preferences and capacities

The surrounding circles of others can reflect back responses to self-presentations in ways that can increase a sense of coherent identity. Such containment and reflection are prominent in the psychoanalytic understanding of individual and group therapy situations. As Bion (1997) has pointed out, the therapeutic alliance can function so as to help patients feel safely contained, freer than when alone to explore usually warded-off emotional themes and dissociated but potentially activated self-states.

When a therapeutic message is offered to a patient, it is contained in this safe situation even when the remark points out a pattern that is not advantageous. However, such a remark can also be taken as an insult. The patient is parallel processing what is happening in the present moment in the social situations and may shift role-relationship models so that one model has a safer self and a protective surrounding, and another model has a vulnerable self surrounded with possible critics out to embarrass the individual. Person schemas theory helps us understand how both models may be operative at the same time, and the person may oscillate between feeling helped and insulted even when the intent is therapeutic.

In other words, a person comes to therapy with a repertoire of selves contained in a repertoire of role-relationship models. The best fit of the role-relationship models to the actual therapy situation starts a therapeutic alliance. Experiences in the alliance reshape the schemas in a direction that increases understanding and a sense of safety. As safety increases, risks can be taken. Other role-relationship models may be activated, contained in the safer ones. Transference projections may occur and may be reappraised in reflective self-awareness.

The safe social situation of good therapy helps advance supra-ordinate self-schemas, thereby enhancing personality functioning and promoting identity growth. Any good quality in a new experience, especially feeling understood because of apt empathy, can promote advances in self-definition. Social reflectance is important to self-maintenance in a changing body and a changing world.

Conclusion

Psychological, conscious, and unconscious development of self-organization occurs in a relational matrix. A two-person, self–other system of core attachments is itself contained in larger and larger social groups and ecological contexts. Larger systems feed information back and forth to smaller systems of meaning.

Roles for the individual are prominently affected in an inter-generational way. New and old modes of being a self, and having a role with others, are both offered and constricted by tradition and modern socio-economic conditions. The result is a complex play of social forces always influencing the possible self-states of an individual.

Chapter 5

Biological schematization

Networks and modular brain connectivity

Modern neuroscience has shown us how complex the brain is in its structure and function. Person schemas function to organize the top end of this complexity. Person schemas, especially ones for self-organization and self–other attachments, connect networks and modules for social information processing.

In turn, the maintenance and revision through learning from new relationship experiences depend on late-evolving neural networks. If such neural networks do not evolve adequately, then it will be harder to develop supra-ordinate self-schemas in adulthood. Even if such capacities were gained, say, in one's twenties and thirties, and are subsequently lost, as in senile dementia or other brain damage, then in such situations identity and relationship functioning may regress.

The level of person schematic functioning in the present moment may vary with activity, for example, in the activity of a network of associations that produces a self-state. This activity at the neurophysiological level organizes what happens in networks that produce conscious self–other thoughts, fantasies, and interpersonal actions, as well as the here-and-now characteristics of emotional expression and regulation. High levels of identity and relationship functioning take the building blocks of lower levels of brain neural activity and reorganize the units of information into complex cognitive maps such as role-relationship models.

In other words, brain modules and network linkages are hierarchical just as, at the psychological and social levels, knowledge is hierarchical. Subordinate integrations are nested into supra-ordinate integrations, as sets of information are processed back and forth, up and down, from more unitized to more differentiated and complex functioning.

The highest level of integration, in effect, reconsiders lower sets of information over time, not just now, but in relation to the past, and in having expectations of and intentions for the future. These higher-level connectivities determine aptness in social transactions and a sense that, in effect, answers the psychological question: "Will the 'I' have continuity, and will 'it, the me' endure?"

Self-referencing

People remember self-referential information better than other type of information; information involving self is highly emotionally evocative (Watson,

Dritschel, Obonsawin, & Jentzsch, 2007). Reduction in capacity for establishing such connectivity can lead to alarming disturbances in a person's sense of identity, and to states characterized by under-regulated emotionality. Temporo-frontal deficits make such alarming self-states more likely when the person perceives sources of stress. The increase in perceived stress can further disorganize optimum thinking capacities, and lead to under-modulated states of mind

Neuroplasticity and learning from new bodily and relationship experiences

New associations that are created between sets of information, and repeated over time, lead to changes in synaptic strength. The prefrontal cortex, especially, displays a dynamic sequence of maturation of gray matter, with pruning of non-gray matter, and some synapses. The improved connectivity is probably associated with changed self-schematization (Gogtay et al., 2004).

New attitudes are formed and these new attitudes then operate to organize information. The neuroplasticity occurs in a range: from conditioned associations at lower levels of information processing, to more complexity in episodic memory and generalization into schemas, and to identity and relationship attitudes at the highest levels of associational connectivities. The entire range is involved in new learning from new relationship experiences.

People with higher-level schemas from prior experiences may be the most proficient at new learning. Higher-level neural connectivities may have made it possible to learn more about self and other attachments in both early development, and in the present. If high-level information transactions were impaired by brain-based limitations or deficiencies, these same connectivities may never have occurred.

Synaptic plasticity allows a person to learn from new experiences. This learning can heal painful self-schemas such as "I am bad," developed perhaps in the context of childhood traumatic experiences, and help develop healthier, more bearable meanings. For people without negative self-schemas, synaptic plasticity promotes the development of maturity through learning new skills for novel tasks, and for adapting flexibly to changing life demands. Down-regulation of limbic emotional systems from higher-level person schematizing systems may be improved (Ofen, 2012).

Anatomy of self-recognitions

To recapitulate what was just said in terms of the self-experience of a self-state, that possibly conscious self-reflective awareness is the result of a stacked-up assembly of neural activities from simple non-conscious notations of information as "of the self" to conscious assemblies of images, words, or kinesthetic representations that can function as new appraisals, interpretations and, thus, possible revision of core attitudes. The prefrontal cortex is the seat of this highest level of self-understanding and the nesting of self in relation to person schematizations of important others and communities (D'Argembeau et al., 2012).

Various brain studies have shown that the right and medial prefrontal cortices process information about the self (Platek, Keenan, Gallup, & Mohamed, 2004). These may connect with a default mode network that is involved in the self-coding of information. In the higher connections, and across modes, person schematizations of self and other, and relationships between them as in attachments, are enduring forms of association between subordinate memories and memory generalizations (Moran, Kelley, & Heatherton, 2013). Once again, the argument here is that the current activity of self-schemas organizes the complex information that may feed into conscious awareness and rational thought.

Brain location of alternative "selves"

Treatment of severe epilepsy once required the surgical cutting of the two main tracts that communicate between the brain's right and left cortices. Sperry (1974) studied patients after they had undergone this procedure. He did this by giving them stimuli delivered by optical devices to either the right, or the left, hemisphere. The hemispheres did not communicate, as they would have done before the surgery. In fact, the patients responded to the stimuli as if they had almost different senses of identity, in the moment. Nonetheless, the common folk wisdom of right and left brains is usually oversimplified. Networks of synaptic connections cross hemispheres, back and forth, to achieve higher levels of self and relationship understanding. Parallel and distributive processing can proceed unconsciously, by many coding systems, in higher and higher levels of organization of meanings. Alternative selves in multiple personality are like the self-states discussed in previous chapters. The alternatives are activations of complex networks of associations, and shifts are activations of some of the same nodes but different overall combinations of network unit activations.

Person schemas as organizers of parallel distributive processing in social cognition

Different self-schemas can organize different streams of information appraisal, proceeding unconsciously and in parallel channels of organized information. Activation of person schemas, such as roles of relationship in known attachments to others, can foster predictions of what is likely to happen. Different role-relationship models between self and other might be simultaneously activated. The output of these channels, operating in parallel time, can lead to different interpretations—and so, to different potential emotional reactions—of the self-and-relationship meanings of new situations. The best output would most likely be the result of using the special problem-solving tools that conscious reflection can provide.

These high-level appraisals and organizations by person schematization are believed to involve cortical midline structures of the cortex and sub-cortex, and down-regulating: the controlling arousal of lower-level motivational and emotional networks, such as the limbic systems. Northoff and Bermpohl (2004) suggest that cortical midline structures, such as the orbitomedial prefrontal cortex, are crucial to processing self-referential stimuli. Also, regions such as the precuneus, the ventral striatum, and the subgenual anterior cingulate cortex are involved in the reorganization of self-relevant information (Rameson, Satpute, & Lieberman, 2010). A related system is called *interoception*.

Interoception literally means perception of the inside of the body. The insula cortex, located beneath the lateral sulcus, between the temporal and parietal lobes, collects such information and, after collating it, moves organized information to all the networks of the brain. Studies utilizing functional magnetic resonance imaging (fMRI) can examine excitations of networks in short order slices of time. The data gathered suggests that the insula cortex functions to compare and contrast current, past, or expected future states of the self (Craig, 2004, 2008; Olausson et al., 2005). While this area may be highly involved, it cannot handle the complexity of self-organizational continuity alone. To repeat the main point: person schemas can organize how complex and dynamical systems connect and transact (Berlin, 2011; Zelner, 2011; Kandel, 2012).

Comparisons of sets of information—involving the insula—are vital to informing identity. These comparisons recognize what is and isn't part of the self. They can examine plans for action, such as: what can the body do or not do? For instance, some children, or even adolescents, make errors after watching superhero movies or wrestling stunts on TV. These young people imagine they can fly, and do not accurately assess the body's real inability to do so. They may compare ideal with real, or real with dreaded projections of what the body can do.

The insula cortex can signal mismatches that, at the psychological level of transduction of information, can be felt as an emotional arousal. Mismatches, perhaps between this view of self and another view, motivate information processing in order to reach some kind of accord. A recent event or a possible future plan is reconsidered in terms of threat, opportunity, and needs of the self. This does not mean that the insula is the seat of emotional potentials, but rather, that signals from it might activate other emotional arousal sites (Rasch et al., 2009).

Mirror neurons: processing other-related information within self-systems

Mirror neurons have been a popularized aspect of neuroscience. The finding that excites public interest is that the brain's "self" can simulate what may be happening in the minds of others by means of using perceptions of the other as if they were self-sensations. When one perceives a person being stuck with a pin in the arm, for instance, one lights up brain networks that are in similar areas as when pain is felt in one's own arm. Mirror neurons serve an intermediary function.

The information, at brain level, functions to promote a model of what is happening, to some extent, in another person's brain. The result at higher levels may relate to capacities for empathic resonance, which could in turn promote adroit social cognitions (Fonagy, 2001). The highest process may use such information as a part of learning by identification.

Genetics and brain development

The anatomy and physiological propensities of the brain form from genetically coded information, as modified by intrauterine life and subsequent sub-gene changes in chemistry and activation. Genes or snips of genes can be modified by epigenetic expressions, probably at any time in adult life. That is why Kendler and colleagues use the apt term, referring to a "developmentally dynamic genome" (2008). Toxicity, stress, trauma, and chemical stimulations can evoke a different expression of genes than might otherwise occur. That will affect brain network functioning and at the highest levels of complexity influence identity.

In other words, in the brains of affected individuals, polymorphisms take place in many genes. Multiple snips may interact to produce different proteins at the pre- and post-synaptic junctions. Tract connectivities might be impaired with some changes, possibly leading to loss of the highest level of schematizing functioning, and so toward identity disturbances.

Many areas of disturbed neural network functioning could impair accurate self-appraisals, appraisals of others, conceptual separations of self and other, and appropriate knowledge of enduring and reliable attachments with others. When the highest levels of self-organization are not attained, or, if attained once, cannot currently be maintained, then alarms about the self are more likely to occur, and a self-protective coping stance may resemble paranoid thinking to others. That is, the individual may exhibit a tendency to see others as dangerously hard to understand, or menacing potential predators. And such an individual is more likely to experience his or her emotional self as mysteriously fluctuating and so dangerously hard to control.

Chemistry

Oxytocin is a hormone released by the pituitary gland that stimulates the ejection of milk into the ducts of a mother's nursing breasts. It has many other effects. Research using nasal spray of this substance may show some increase in social reciprocity, a change in self-state. It may also intensify rejection of outsiders by insider groups to which the self feels more belonging. Of course, many other substances are involved in augmenting or reducing social awareness and identity.

Some television commercials for drugs have popularized the term "chemical imbalance" and there may be salience to the concept. Persons with kinds of depression that are believed to be related somehow to serotonin fluctuations have identity disturbances that are characterized by self-degradation, and difficulties in finding relationship satisfaction. Ingested substances, autoimmune antibodies, and high stress on hormonal systems can alter the brain functioning, and even the brain structure. Localized disease can produce neurological conditions. Diffuse problems, such as disorders of the spaces between cells of the brain—in the intercellular fluid where chemicals swim especially actively—would be likely to impair the highest level of network connectivity functioning in information processing, therefore, also impairing self and relationship appraisals and/or maintenance of person-schematizing maps. Current abilities at self and other appraisal and understanding might decline from prior levels of higher capacities (Muenchberger, Kendall, & Neal, 2008).

Consider a previously healthy person who, after consuming too much methamphetamine (dexedrine, speed), develops identity disturbances, paranoid suspiciousness, and hostility toward others. These disorders of thinking are based on deterioration in functional brain capacity for putting together accurate self–other information. The highest levels of complex processing are the ones most likely to be disrupted first, leading to wrong appraisals of self-attributes as a first sign of what could go on to impede lower levels of brain function (Morishita & Aihara, 2004). If that person, before taking the drug, was vulnerable to lapses in self-esteem or self-coherence due to early developmental impairments in self and other schematization, then he or she would be more likely to abuse substances to ameliorate distress, and to have more deterioration as a consequence of addiction.

Biopsychosocial integration

Social stress and emergent psychological conflicts can affect brain activity. For example, company layoffs may elicit a multitude of responses in employees. Normal stress responses can lead to attention focusing, motivational commitment, and positive coping in many who then seek new jobs and maintain their self-esteem. Some members of this social group will have higher stress, more fear, diminished self-esteem and bitterness. The higher stress will affect brain activity, irrational thinking or giving up may occur. A sense of sorrow, worthlessness, or rage may lead to further loss of support from taking frustrations out on coworkers or family members. Past memories of parental disputes over finances or catastrophic losses, long dormant, can be re-activated. The person imagines total abandonment and a helpless self-schema may be activated.

The activation of incompetent self-schemas combined with the blow of job loss and economic strain seems even more catastrophic in terms of any future plans, and transacts with the fatigue and loss of clear thinking capacities from disruption of the highest levels of network connectivity due to prolonged stress hormones and neurotransmitters. Neural damage may even occur. The totality can limit the capacities for down-regulation of anxiety circuitry. A vicious cycle continues as any further bad news leads to excessively high alarm reactions. Applied social support can reduce alarms and repair the brain equilibrium, leading to better coping. The bio, the psycho, and the social all transact, but it takes an intact, well-organized brain to cope well.

Conclusion

In its healthy level of functioning, the brain is complex, hierarchical, and integrated. Information is organized across brain networks by connectivities between an incredible number of synapses. The electrochemical and anatomical nature of these synapses retain self and relationship information, over time. This network of information operates as person schematizations. These schemas are organizers of the next information processing that occurs, leading to a variety of self-appraisals and social interactions.

The person schematic matrix of generalized and map-like meanings is limited by the capacities of the growing brain. And, even when fully mature in a healthy, adult brain, the matrix may be degraded by strain, fatigue, and disease. Self-organization, to be harmonized, requires both long development and apt maintenance. When the highest levels of brain connectivity and information transaction are not available, lapses in identity experiences are likely to occur.

Good self-organization and relationship activities are essential to personality functioning, and the levels of disturbance in personality functioning that result from lack of harmonization are the topic of Chapter 6.

Personality functioning

Levels of person schematic organization and variations in psychotherapy technique

Does a person seem to have stable affiliations and self-esteem, or disturbances in identity and relationships? An observer's placement of an individual along this range is an estimate of the subject's level of personality functioning. Such inferences about self-organization and attachment attitudes are important to clinicians because, as a continuing aspect of case formulation, the results are likely to lead to an apt selection of treatment techniques that, in the present phase of change, are most likely to foster personality growth.

In most psychotherapies the patient and clinician both learn in the context of a conversational sequence. The verbal statements of each party to the dyad is embodied in a non-verbal, growingly secure, and progressively clarified framework usually called a therapeutic alliance. The patient learns from the new sensory, perceptual, and verbally represented experiences within the relationship. Learning also results from the patient's new work and experiences with outside relationships.

Along this way to learning new schematizations from more rewarding experiences, the therapist, in a major additional process, is also helping the patient develop better information-processing skills. The patient is learning and also learning how to learn. An important component of these skills involves learning how to enhance and more often use reflective self-awareness. Enhancing self-reflective awareness increases the regulation of self-states and emotional expressions. This progresses into rich, novel, interpersonal experiences.

Patients at different levels of person schematization, in a given phase of therapy, are able to use the attention-focusing efforts of the therapist in different ways. Patients with lower levels of self-organization, those with relative deficiencies in supra-ordinate self-schemas, find it harder to process complex pattern clarifications and interpretations. They have not yet learned the higher skills of self-reflection and emotional self-regulation. Parallel processing of relationship views, as in comparing role-relationship models used to organize a recent conversation, is too difficult for them.

For example, if the therapist is asking for a comparison and contrast between alternative role-relationship views, and self-states, then the patient is more likely to become confused as to what the therapist's verbal statement meant.

This chapter aims to examine that proposition in which the therapist must not overwhelm the patient with excessively complex conceptualizations. The therapist aims to prevent destabilization of the patient's self-states either from excessive emotional arousal of affects such as rage or intense transferences such as erotized longing.

Unfortunately, the adage, "the rich get richer and the poor get poorer," may also apply to relationship learning opportunities. People who are inept at appraising self and others find it harder, in a good-enough therapeutic situation, to develop a safe and continuing relationship, one usually called a *therapeutic alliance,* because that kind of relationship correlates so well with improvements in symptoms and problems (Krupnick, 2001). Now, a patient with lifelong disturbances in self and relationship schemas can slowly learn a new experience of trust, consistency, and acceptance; new experience can advance the patient's level of personality functioning (Bion, 1957; Winnicott, 1958; Morey et al., 2011).

Therapists can augment their technique by knowing how to assess the degree of coherence between self-states in the current functioning of a patient. While they will not find this to be an easy task, the level of such functioning is important, as shown by research on the interaction of process and outcome. Clinical studies have shown that therapy techniques useful at promoting improvements in patients at higher levels of personality functioning may not be helpful to those patients who operate at lower levels of personality functioning, and vice versa (Horowitz, Marmar, Weiss, DeWitt, & Rosenbaum, 1984; Piper et al., 1991b; Millon, 1999; Blatt, Auerbach, & Levy 1997; Høglend et al., 2006; Gamache et al., 2009; Diener & Monroe, 2011; Mullin & Hilsenroth, 2012).

Levels of person schematic functioning: self-states and relationship patterns

Levels of personality functioning can be defined as follows: the current capacities of a person for using inner working models to make apt choices and have realistic experiences in the area of self-definition and interpersonal choices. These capacities are based on enduring person schemas, including self-schemas and role-relationship models. This definition is in accord with the proposed Level of Personality Functioning Scale (LPFS) that a task force prepared for potential use in *DSM-V* (Bender, Morey, & Skodol, 2011). Skodol and colleagues (2011) and Zimmerman et al. (2012) define the five levels to be rated by clinicians in complex tables of possible inferences using headings of identity, self-direction, empathy, and intimacy. The final board rejected the LPFS for the main diagnostic section II of *DSM-5*. Along with personality trait dimensions and new typologies, they relegated the LPFS to section III, a place for variables that might be utilized in future research.

The Level of Personality Functioning Scale prepared by that taskforce had a great potential for predictive validity. It resembled the Organizational Levels of Self and Other Schematization (OLSOS) developed in our University of California San Francisco research group, with NIMH funding, and developed further within the person schemas task force of the MacArthur Program on Conscious and Unconscious Mental Processes (Horowitz et al., 1984, Horowitz, 1991, 1998). Like the LPFS colleagues, we found that a dimensional approach to scoring level of personality functioning required complexity. That meant scoring required interviewing with clinical expertise. From that information we found that the ratings were best kept simple and we used, as on the LPFS, five levels from 0 as coherent self-organization to 4 to more disturbance. Table 6.1 summarizes the potential observations for making these inferences.

Table 6.1 Levels of integration of self–other schematization

Level	Description
Harmonious	Internal desires, needs, frustrations, impulses, choices, and values are appraised as "of the self." Realistic pros and cons are examined to reach choices of rational action and restraint. Grounded in self, one views others as separate people with their own intentions, expectations, and emotional reactions. Perspectives on relationships approximate social realities. Past and present views of self and relationships are integrated, allowing a sense of constancy and modification of ambivalence. State transitions are smooth, appropriate, and adroit. Warm and caring relationships are maintained over time in spite of episodic frustrations. Emotional governance prevents out-of-control states.
Mildly conflicted	While good-enough relationships are formed in his or her closest work and intimate affiliations, the person displays states that contain varied intentions, manifesting as conflicting approach and distancing tendencies. On examination, these alternations are based on fluctuating attitudes about self in the relationship. Most commonly, fears of rejection may limit warm and caring attachments to others, or fears of subordination limit high levels of cooperation. The person appraises self with a variety of critical judgments: some too harsh, some too lax. State transitions occur between positive and negative moods, but the shifts in state are remembered and not explosive surprises or emergence of alternative selves.
Vulnerable	A sense of self-regard deteriorates under stress, criticism, and increased pressures to perform. To protect from feelings of inferiority or enfeeblement, grandiose supports of self-esteem may be utilized. Concern for the well-being of others may be considered less important than using others as tools for self-enhancement. Surprising shifts from vigor and boldness to states of apathy, boredom, or unpleasant restlessness may occur. Because of insufficient self-organization, the person may shift between being loving; suddenly, overly demanding; and suddenly appeasing. Emotional governance is reduced. Undermodulated rage may erupt at others who are perceived as insulting and are blamed for otherwise shameful deflations in the individual's own self-esteem.

(Continued)

Table 6.1 (Continued)

Level	Description
Disturbed	Life seems organized by using various self-states, and some of them seem like a break with reality. Errors in self–other attribution occur. Undesirable self-attributes and emotions are projected from self to other. The actions of self may be confused in memory in terms of who did or felt what, and shifts in self-state may be accompanied by apparent forgetting of what happened in the alternative state of mind. Memories frequently combine fantasies with once-real elements. State transitions can be explosive. Dissociative identity experiences re-occur under stress and forgetting and then remembering may occur in segregated states of mind and views of self.
Fragmented	A massive chaos of selfhood can occur and, as a counter to cope with the high distress, the person frequently feels aroused to high defensiveness and accusation of others, as if under attack. As a needed repair of damage to self, the individual may regard self as merged with another person. Or, the person may withdraw in a hibernated, frozen, self-protecting coping effort that, to others, appears bizarre and self-damaging. Parts of the bodily self may be infused with the "badness" and disowned from self-images. This sense of chaos is very painful and can give rise to poorly regulated emotional impulses, including potentially suicidal or homicidal urges, intensified because the strange behaviors lead to social stigmatization.

The labels used for five progressively more disorganized levels of person schematic functioning are: *harmonious*, *mildly conflicted*, *vulnerable*, *disturbed*, and *fragmented*. These labels provide a memory device for communications of what in the past clinicians often spoke of as degree of ego strength, or as levels of integration defined as neurotic character, narcissistic character, borderline character, or psychotic character structure.

Goals for personality growth in treatment

Therapists and patients often have a goal in open-ended psychoanalytic treatments that could be defined as advancement in character structure: increasing identity cohesion and relationship capacities. As mentioned, such personality growth can occur in the context of a safe relationship. However, persons at a disturbed level find that the context itself—achieving a safe alliance with a therapist—is unstable.

Patients do not always trust themselves and the therapist together in the therapy situation. Their self-states may vary, and they do not always have a sense of confidence that the felt safety of the relationship framework is enough to contain their potential and dreaded self-states; the self-states are prone to impulsive and intense emotional expressions. Helping the patient develop self-reflective information-processing capacities, and the associated attention control, can increase the sense of safety and that is often the way therapy works to promote change (Sandler & Sandler, 1997).

We can discuss this by first considering change processes induced by therapist interactions with patients who are not highly disturbed, and then progress to considering modifications of technique when treating more disturbed patients.

Self-reflective awareness

One can achieve identity growth by altering erroneous attitudes, re-prioritizing goals, and increasing rational self-definitions. The combination of these learning processes increases self-esteem and self-confidence and promotes better, more satisfying relationships. Since help with self-organization usually occurs in conversational form, patients and therapists need to find a common language for these dialogues. For the patient, this means verbalizing usually intuitive self-concepts and relationship patterns. We will start examining such efforts at self-reflection as promoted by conversations with patients who are observed to be at the more advanced levels of personality functioning, the higher categories defined loosely in Table 6.1.

Even at these mildly conflicted levels of person schematic organization, most people are not used to being frank about disclosing their usually private thoughts and emotions. They tend to keep what they like and dislike in themselves, to themselves. Avoidance is natural, because self-definitions often seem permanent and impossible to change. An idea that change is possible can instill hope: restoring morale counteracts the obstacles presented by proneness to anxious and depressed moods when troublesome topics are examined. This clarification of why therapy is a hopeful opportunity, undertaken by the most competent self-states leads to working-states in which both parties discuss more closely reasoned self-appraisals to counteract fears, hopelessness, and degrading self-criticisms

Clinicians follow the red thread of emotion to reveal underlying attitudes that contain some kind of mismatch between hopes for the self and what actually happens to the self; and mismatches between fears for the self, and what is actually likely to happen. Clinicians help patients name feelings, put self-states in relationship contexts, and clarify beliefs about motives of self and other. That naming process, in and of itself, increases the patient's ability to regulate impulses and emotionality (Fonagy & Target, 1997; Horowitz, 1998, 2005; Kernberg, 2000; Stern, 2004; Young, Klosko, & Weishaar, 2006).

By operating on self-beliefs within stories of interpersonal transactions, a therapist can organize his or her own working models of a patient's pattern of maladaptive relationship transactions. This organization is helped by use of a mapping sentence that specifies the patient's sense of "I," as suggested by Luborsky (1984). The therapist can say something based on the mapping sentence: "You felt (emotion naming) when the other person seemed (naming the other's actions or expressed feelings) and your reaction was (naming emotional response of self). The consequence was further self-evaluation, such as self-criticism, leading to shame."

If the patient is in a self-state with some reflective awareness, the multiple points in the therapist's pattern clarifications can then be compared and contrasted, leading toward new reasoning. If the patient absorbs the clarifications, he or she learns that the therapist has empathic understanding. The patient learns to put attitudes and moods into words. The patient also learns the therapist's role in a therapeutic alliance. Gradually, identification occurs, perhaps with the therapist's calm stance of trying to understand what is happening. This combination leads to an enhancement of the patient's self-reflective awareness.

Clarification

A lot of therapy involves the therapist deciding where to focus the joint attention of the conversational duo, and the process usually starts with a clarification. The clarifications made by the therapist, as remarks, may restate the beliefs of the patient. The therapist rearranges concepts and memories to show cause-and-effect sequences. By clarifying, the therapist is advancing toward interpretation; the interpretations might compare and contrast a patient's dysfunctional beliefs with more realistic views. If needed, the developmental origin of currently dysfunctional beliefs might be interpreted (Strupp, 1980, 1993).

Lucid verbalization of self-criticisms is an important aspect of such work. Many clarifications found in content analyses of transcripts of useful therapy sessions involve the therapist restating a patient's own self-judgment on a feeling that the patient has expressed. A typical clarification is illustrated in the following case example of Ms. P.

Ms. P was a 29-year-old, single, Caucasian female living alone in an apartment. She had been employed for the past six years as a high school teacher, and had no close friends. She went to a singles bar, met a man, and went outside to talk with him. In the parking lot, he sexually assaulted her. Getting into her own car, she went home without consulting a doctor or the police. She stated that she was attempting to "just go on with her life."

She came for treatment, months later, for a stress response syndrome characterized by flashback memories, loneliness, low self-esteem, nightmares, avoidance of social connections, and intrusive daytime preoccupation with whether or not to go out on dates. Her symptoms diminished rapidly with the establishment of an agreement on weekly psychotherapy.

After initial state stabilization, the therapy was aimed toward a process that could help her to integrate her various self-schemas. She worked toward more self-coherence, self-agency in planning her life, and how to choose healthier relationships. Ms. P tried to understand how she impulsively acted with sometimes-dangerous men: to get too deep into bonding, too early.

Her mid-therapy reviews of the trauma memory meant reconsidering what she'd thought, in making the decision to go off alone, with a relative stranger. In one such session, she retold the sequence:

Ms. P: You felt less alone even with him smiling at you. You didn't want to be left alone. You wanted to stay with him. So you go outside hoping it will work out. Crazy. It sure didn't!

Therapist: I know you feel self-critical in retrospect, but you use a language in which you were saying "you," telling me what I might experience in that situation, rather than using the word for yourself, "I." What we are doing is learning from this story as we review it together, and what you said gives me an empathic feeling for how you felt and still feel. And I wonder what it might feel like, repeating a bit, reflecting on your feelings, if you were to say what you just did, only saying "I" rather than "you?"

This is a long remark. It is an experiment to see what kinds of clarifications can help the patient in this phase of her treatment in processing the memory. If the clarification works well, the patient is thinking all along, in each phrase that she heard from the therapist. She stays with what the therapist means, self-reflecting on reactions in her mind in the present moment, feeling and shaping thoughts that might clarify her self-concepts, her self-as-inner-critic, and her interpersonal attitude. If the experiment fails to approach such goals, if the patient goes into a harsh state of self-bashing without reflection, then the optimum processing that might modify her dysfunctional beliefs and schemas is not available.

Clinicians know that therapy deepens as a helping alliance creates a more pervasive sense of safety. Until then, a patient may be testing the waters to see if embarrassment and disorganization can be avoided while emotional frankness is increased. The process begins with clarification, often by consideration of current crises and provocations from outside the mind. Examining cause and consequences leads to examining choices of how to cope with repetitions. As safety is augmented, the conversation deepens to clarifications of patterns. This eventually leads below the surface, to progressive examination of core attitudes and possibly interpretations about their probable formation in early development.

Along the way, the patient encounters and counteracts obstacles, avoidance patterns, and mechanisms of defense that have become habitual. A repertoire of self-states that are desired, dreaded, and defensively avoided, may then be clarified.

This progression from surface to depth occurs faster in persons at higher levels of current personality functioning. Higher-functioning patients can compare and contrast the clarified scenarios, thus differentiating reality from fantasy, and revising outmoded life stories with new interpretations and personal narratives. Patients at lower levels of current personality functioning demonstrate more difficulty in conversational understanding, and are likely to get lost in just one part of the whole picture.

Approaching maladaptive attitudes

Interpretation of how a repetitive, maladaptive, interpersonal pattern impairs personality functioning is a classical technique. The interpretation may include clarification of the pattern, how and why it developed at an earlier time, and its future consequences, if not modified. The therapist may help the patient to modify the outdated attitudes.

Various methods for the formulation of such patterns have been shown to be reliable (Horowitz, 1991; Eells, 2007). These methods include: the *Core Conflictual Relationship Theme* of Luborsky and Crits-Christoph (1990), the *Structural Analysis of Social Behavior* of Benjamin (2003) and the *Role Relationship Models* component of Configurational Analysis (Horowitz & Eells, 1993; Horowitz, Eells, Singer, & Salovey, 1995; Horowitz, 2005). The consensus on these methods of formulation is identification of self–other roles and transactional beliefs.

Formulation takes repetitions and constructs patterns, focusing on maladaptive beliefs, including self-definitions that are repeated. Self-concepts often emerge as complaints: "I was so stupid!" Such complaints reveal self-criticism but for the patient they are still in an interpersonal matrix, as in a non-verbal stance that if put into words might be: "I want you," i.e. the therapist, "to tell me I was not stupid because that bad episode in my life was that other person's fault." Time on topic usually has to be expanded to get at self-attributions behind the label "stupid."

Sometimes it helps to set up a frame for expanded time when speaking about identity-related topics. Early avoidance of discussing identity-related issues can sometimes be counteracted by asking that conversations have an aim of staying for a time on each of three scenarios, which are all eventually covered. These topics can be announced in advance. In doing so, unconscious processing is set in motion, and attributes of self then are verbalized for conscious reflectance and conversational analysis within each framework.

The three scenarios are: *ideal self-attributes*, *dreaded self-attributes*, and *realistic self-attributes*. These techniques are used for those higher-functioning patients who can use self-reflective awareness to reproduce streams of thought, and to compare and contrast alternative trains of beliefs and feelings. That is, to reappraise the attitudes in various scenarios of how to interpret a social transaction.

Consider, for example, a restless, depressed, and obscure music composer who occupied a stable, salaried position as a professor of music. We can illustrate the various scenarios technique. Responding to each direction of attention from the therapist, his attitudes were revealed. His *ideal self-attribution* was to imagine himself as having great creative talent. His *dreaded self-attribute* was to appraise himself in a degraded way as a silly grandiose imposter who just got by teaching basic musical principles. His *realistic self-attribute* was as a competent teacher of compositional and pianistic techniques, who occasionally wrote good music.

After obtaining the composer's responses to these three scenarios, the therapist asked him to repeat the conversation, going over the same three scenarios and considering, in each, how he expected to be judged by others. This allowed him to examine ideal, dreaded, and real expectations of the opinions of others, as well as to review his own self-appraisals and sources of self-esteem.

The clarifying scenarios approach can be repeated in terms of time frames: how past differs from present, and which different, future selves could be imagined. For example, a 35-year-old woman told me she was once a pretty child, felt her beauty to be fading now, and dreaded being a "hag" with a baggie face by the time she reached 40. This fear, once expressed and reappraised, was seen by her to be an entirely unrealistic expectation that could be modified.

It is crucial to encourage here-and-now, self-as-mature reappraisals during these conversational assessments of attitudes about self. The aim is to differentiate beliefs that are realistic from those that are exaggerated or minimized. The next step is re-prioritizing goals. It is important to emphasize realistic intentions and expectations for the future so that unrealistic goals may be accepted as irrational mental productions, fleeting ideas that may repeat, but not dominate in making choices.

Modifying predictions

Negative attitudes and self-schemas are connected to implicit rules about how people are to behave in life. The price for breaking rules is usually an intuitive assumption of what the consequences might be. One set of possible consequences is a catastrophic prediction. The person expects to be humiliated if she acts boldly, for example.

Such expectations are often anticipated only vaguely, as an intuitively feared outcome. If they are stated as clarifications, in verbal representations, and entered into lucid therapeutic conversations, then such self-degrading assumptions can be painfully submitted to a behavioral test to see if they hold up to reality. For instance, a core belief can be stated: "I am incompetent and actually an imposter in terms of the work skills for which I am employed." From this belief stem particular assumptions about consequences: "if I expose my work products to judgment or criticism I will be fired," therefore, "I will not take professional exposure risks."

A person with such a belief may avoid speaking in a meeting at work, and avoid pursuing a challenging innovation. The imagined catastrophic outcome is challenged in therapy; eventually a plan to test the assumption may be implemented. The patient acts more boldly, according to plan, checking to see if disaster looms—but it does not. The new experience may create new attitudes about self and others. The patient may become bolder in life, finding better results than expected, increasing self-esteem, and reducing depressive and anxious states.

Focusing attention

When a therapist acts verbally or non-verbally, the perception of the therapist alters the patient's deployment of attention. Therapists intuitively know this and are making choices of where to pay more attention. Sometimes, attention may be directed at evaluating two attitudes about self and relationships that conflict.

Conflicts between strong, competent self-views and weak, incompetent self-views are common, and the direction of attention tries to develop some kind of an over-arching harmonization of the contradictory sets of beliefs.

This technique accepts that there may be multiple self-schemas and multiple contradictory attitudes. Higher-level patients have the capacity to use reflective self-awareness to compare and contrast. They can clarify ideas and feelings that can, possibly, revise and articulate beliefs. Words allow patients to develop more complex attitudes to meet truly complex social situations. New attitudes lead toward new trials of behavior. Plans can be modified and repeated. The patient becomes less awkward (because they are doing something new) and more adroit. The repetitions lead to reinforcing satisfactions, and also to new self-schemas.

A committee of selves metaphor

Several sets of self-beliefs emerge from the associational matrix of self-schemas organizing the conversation concerning a specific scenario. Sometimes, putting these together in ideational arrangements is useful: the metaphor of a committee works well. In this metaphor the patient imagines a competent self as the chair of the committee and imagines other types of self-beliefs as personifications that are discussing matters from different points of view (attitudes) while sitting in a circle. They are stating possibly conflicting messages. One self might say, "I want to and deserve to eat all that delights me!" Another self might say, "Over-eating is bad for our health, and you must have more discipline in what you choose to eat." In other words, a conversation about aims can include how to reflect upon wishful and self-critical "parts" of self (Martin, 1997; Mellon, 1998; Siegel, 2010; Horowitz, 2011).

Value stating

Another useful tool—to clarify the derivatives of schemas of self and other that are largely out of awareness—is to ask about values, and to make them a part of the therapeutic dialogue. Values usually pertain to how a person ought to behave, and to differences between an ideal and an actual self-schema. Much has been read about values, and verbalization of them is easier than stating wishes, desires, fears, and dreaded scenarios. However, asking about values means asking after the patient's intuitive sense of right and wrong. This has been a long taboo issue in psychotherapy training because of fears of introducing and thus promoting the therapist's own values.

Putting values into words clarifies what the self believes, and discloses the rules used in forming sometimes too harsh self-criticisms. In such contexts, patients may ask the therapist to state his or her values. The principle of the therapist taking a position of equidistance on all parts of the patient's self, including the possibility of examining value conflicts in the patient, should be explained as an aspect of the boundaries of therapy. The therapist's neutrality serves the aims for therapy, to allow reappraisals and modifications of possibly harsh self-judgments, judgments previously leading to excessive shame or guilt.

By making values explicit, the patient can recognize different goals and contradictions between them. He or she can then prioritize his or her own goals, and take steps to revise unrealistic views of self. Research has shown that commonly useful categories for discussion with patients and research subjects has been to compare attributes of an ideal self, an actual self, and a should-be or ought-to-be self. The ideal self may not be the same as the socially dictated self (Steele, 1988; Singer, 1974; Higgins, 1997). Cultural conflicts, as discussed in Chapter 4, may play a role in the emergent value conflicts.

The discussion of values clarifies self-related conflicts, and can be linked with an examination of how to handle the near future. The questions from the clinician guide the attention in a therapeutic dialogue toward possible steps to avoid self-impairing actions in reacting to current moral dilemmas, or making amends for previous mis-deeds. In resolving remorse, wishes for revenge, or a tendency to excessive harsh self-appraisals, it is important to reduce perfectionistic attitudes. This often leads to modifications of attitudes based on childhood or adolescent imperatives toward achieving fame, genius levels of creativity, or being rewarded for extraordinary bodily feats.

Let me recapitulate the main points made so far. Therapists clarify and interpret beliefs that are dysfunctional. Usually, these are attitudes that pertain to self as conceptualized in a relationship, a relationship that has schematic scenarios with particular transactive patterns, including potentials for the emotions to be felt at points within the scenario by each party. These patterns can be seen as action, response, and reaction leading toward previously maladaptive consequences. The therapist wants to help the patient avoid that same consequence, in the future.

The therapist wants to aid reflective self-awareness by comparisons of adaptive and maladaptive attitudes. These comparisons may be too difficult to accomplish for some patients, in the midst of distressing emotional conversations with the therapist. In some self-states, found more often at disturbed levels, a patient may experience clarification of a dysfunctional belief as if the therapist were attacking or at least insulting her. A disturbed level individual may take a suggested change in ideas to mean that something is wrong with his or her self, in a global sense. The patient may believe that the therapist is saying, "You are bad," possibly re-enacting a message he or she heard repeatedly in early childhood.

Shorter, more tactful messages are needed. Therapy goes more slowly with disturbed self-organizational issues because of the recurrent need to stabilize a safe therapeutic relationship. Clinicians find that it is generally best to proceed carefully with schema-uncovering work with such patients, as activation of schemas of the self, as assaulted or even persecuted, can produce a self-state with a flood of overwhelming negative emotions (Piper et al., 1991b; Diener & Monroe, 2011).

Techniques for patients with disturbed and fragmented self-states

Some individuals at very disturbed levels of identity and relationship functioning have self-states in which the endangered self is struggling with tyrannical inner presences, a not-self attacking its own mind, or even its own body. That internal mental presence is neither part of experienced identity nor is it quite an image of another person. A therapist is outside this not-self but can be seen as a threatening presence, like a part of self that operates as an inner, harsh, punitive critic.

If and when this loss of safety occurs, hostility is in the air; predation is expected. Anything the therapist says may, in the emotional turmoil of such states, be mis-perceived as an attack. There is a danger that, to protect a threatened self, the patient may launch physical hostility. The goal is to counteract this by speaking of how best to be an ally to the beleaguered, enfeebled, or fragile self. At the same time, the reactive hostility of the patient's voice or facial expression may make the patient seem very strong and menacing, and the therapist may need to be aware of his or her own discomfort with implied physical threats, on the one hand, and feeling shut-out and worthless, on the other hand (Kernberg, 2000).

Self-protection—by externalizing bad attributes, such as being to blame for harm or neglect—is common when persons at lower levels of personality func-tioning are criticized, frustrated, and pressured. When stressful topics are brought into joint reflection, the patient's endangered self-states may emerge. The safety of a felt alliance with a caring therapist may fluctuate from presence to absence, and back and forth. This may lead to patients projecting predation, contempt, or anger onto their inner view of the therapist, or even provoke the therapist into negative reactions toward them—sometimes called projective identification (Klein, 1948).

When the patient is at lower levels of personality functioning, in fragile self-states, the therapist proceeds slowly, tactfully, and in small doses of clarification: usually stating a clarification of just one element of what is happening, and reviewing what seems to be going on, moment by moment, waiting until the patient is ready for more extensive processing of attitudes and emotions.

People with lower levels of self–other schematization have many contradictions across self-concepts and attitudes about their roles in relationships. They tend to introduce distortions of attribution into treatment relationships just as they do when they re-enact erroneous patterns of attribution outside of therapy. This is transfer-ence, but patients at lower levels of personality functioning may not have sufficient conceptual skills for interpretations that compare the projections of transference with the actualities of the therapeutic alliance offered by the therapist.

With a higher-functioning patient, the therapist may compare a transference-type of role-relationship model with the therapist's clarification of the roles of the patient and therapist in their existing therapeutic alliance. Even with such "let's compare and contrast" efforts by the therapist, even with accurate formu-lations of the transference attitudes, even with many preparatory clarifications, lower-functioning patients may explode into moods in which they regard the helping clinician as intending an attack or aiming toward an imminent abandonment. They cannot hold the transference model and the alliance model in conscious reflecting at the same time.

For example, in mid-therapy, Ms. P had a separation from a new potentially intimate relationship, when she became anxious over his physical overtures. Then she experienced a depressive state that worried her therapist:

Therapist: You have been distressed and seem to me to perhaps be preoccupied with rather hopeless and helpless thoughts. I suggest that we might consider increasing your sessions from once to twice a week for a while.

Ms. P: (*angrily and explosively*) You are saying I am too needy. You react just like he feels about me, too needy, too needy for him to stick with, so you think another hour can do something! One hour more in a whole week! You are full of it! Where do you get off judging me!?

A therapist might be tempted to back off saying, "No, I'm not judging you. I know you are capable. I was just concerned." A potential problem with this remark is that it may sound defensive. Or a therapist might challenge her anger, "Why is it that you are so angered about what I said? What is it about what I said that suggested that I think you are incapable?" By this remark, he would hopefully address her possible projections of an abusive controlling intention. The patient may not be able to recall what the therapist said that angered her. A third alternative response might be, "I irritated you" (pause for non-verbal signs of attention), "I didn't mean to irritate you by what I said." This remark clarifies what is happening and the therapist's intentions in staying within the framework of a therapeutic alliance.

A therapist's goal, when working with a patient at a low level of current self-and-relational organization, is to help the patient gain coherence between self-states. This work is slow. To repeat: the therapist aims at assisting the patient by aiding a process of new attitude formation, doing so by repeating simple clarifications, making small tactful challenges of unrealistic attitudes, while sometimes stating, in calm moments, realistic appraisals.

The negative effects of perceived critics

Any kind of criticism perceived by a patient as coming from a therapist can be detrimental to processes that might lead to good treatment outcomes (Strupp, 1993). Self-criticism can be so harsh that it feels like an internal attack on the mind itself. A patient may unconsciously deflect the judgment, feeling as if the attack comes from outside the self. A projection of blame occurs.

Externalization of the source of criticism supplies a narrative to support a "you are bad, not I" position. Giving interpretations to promote insight about maladaptive attitudes at the wrong time can stop progress in the therapy. The therapist's remarks, however accurate, feel like criticism to the patient. Even gaining insight can lead to self-criticism (as a form of the inner attack on the mind, pitting one part of self against another part).

When critical attack is "in the air," the therapist may use clarification to heighten awareness of a trustworthy therapeutic alliance. If the therapist succeeds in evoking a renewed sense of safety, then rational discourse may improve. The therapist is teaching the patient in a deliberate manner, with explanation, that ideas are being examined, meanings are being negotiated, cooperation is happening.

A patient acquires enhanced capacities for reflective self-awareness gradually, oscillating between progress and retreat, through recognition of the therapist's stance, and acquiring such roles through identification with the calm way in which the clinician works. The patient learns how to repeat what happens in a dialogue. The patient learns how, with each repetition, to clarify each person's intention in a transactional sequence.

The therapist's experience of the patient's attitudes and feelings, as projected onto the therapist, with the patient seeming to experience negative emotions as coming from the therapist, can be a distressing moment for most therapists. That is why therapists usually try to address hostility and criticism early, as occurring in some intermediate conceptual space between themselves and their patients; they try to help their patients see that what seems to patients like a conflict between therapist and patient, or even hostility located by the patient as if inside the therapist, is actually a conflict between "parts of self" inside the patient's mind (Feldman, 2007).

For example, Ms. P was periodically in a frustrated, lost, and empty-self-feeling state of mind. While it was distressing in and of itself, she hated that she entered such states, and hated herself for being vulnerable enough to enter into such states. An inner critic "self" of Ms. P might attack her weak, potentially dependent self-mind; or she could externalize, becoming that critic, and attack the therapist. Attacking the therapist made her feel stronger. It had the added function, for her, of testing to see if the therapist would abandon her: it would be reassuring if he stayed with her, attempting to contain the hostility in the air. Unconsciously, she feared such abandonment and she hoped he would not terminate her, but such an interpretation would have been premature in the self-state operating in organizing this interchange:

Ms. P (sarcastically):   Yes, doctor, you have been supportive, and increasing to twice a week, how kind, how very kind of you. Well, that only makes me more tragically dependent on you, you probably like that, and you just want to get more money from my insurance.

Therapist: (*calmly*) Um hmmm.

Ms. P: You are just another self-aggrandizing exploiter who seems nice, but probably hates women.

Therapist:	Just like abusive males in your past.
Ms. P:	Whatever. Go ahead, you must have your way.
Therapist:	Criticism is in the air, and I know you do not like being perceived by anyone, even yourself, as being vulnerable just because you want to feel connected and less lonely.
Ms. P:	Yadda, yadda, yadda, Dr. Psychobabble … (*withdraws, stares off glassy-eyed into space*)
Therapist:	Hey, what I said got us nowhere, I agree. I should have said that there is a lot of frustration and blaming in the air, right now. My bet is that we can agree on that.

Ms. P enters a contemplative silence. She commences hostile staring at the therapist, and then silently looks at the therapist's face, dropping her hostile expression.

This last remark from the therapist may be advantageous. It labels feelings in words and encourages further exploration rather than quick externalization of blame. Aided by the therapist's clarifications and safety-supporting offer of an alliance, Ms. P was learning to slow down and down-regulate the intensity of her anger in the moment.

Steiner (1994) has pointed out that some disturbed patients may enter a treatment state of mind in which they do not wish to understand themselves. As in the above example, such patients may experience a therapist's efforts toward such understanding as unwelcome and even appraise it as having a hostile intention. Such patients, however, are motivated by a wish that the therapist understand them. Instead of giving interpretations and using "you" words in addressing patients when they are in such self-states, therapists can increase a feeling of safety and the presence of a therapeutic alliance by a willingness to explain what is in the therapist's own mind. And, from such interventions, the patient may learn by identification and new relationship experiences, rather than insight from clarifications and interpretations.

Projections

In persons with more disturbed personality functioning, therapists may find that projections are more frequent, including projections onto the therapist. What is happening in projections? A self-attribution, in a schema that the patient wants to de-activate, appears in the patient's conscious mind as if it were an attribute of the therapist and not the self.

For example, suppose there has been a self-state of the patient in which he or she organizes the conversation by a role-relationship model. In this model, the self-schema is a somewhat dependent "learning" adult, receiving help from a respected expert concerning useful concepts about what the individual can become. At the same time, what is going on in the conversation is, in a kind of parallel processing, being viewed by a self-schematic stance, as a part-self envying the part-self that is having a good alliance—perhaps because of previous grievances at not having had such help from either parent, as is now being experienced with the therapist, The hostility can emerge if and when this envy emerges. The part-selves are not united within a supra-ordinate self-organization, as discussed in Chapter 3.

A shift from too weak to strong self-states may occur. In a bizarre-appearing state of mind, perhaps one startling the therapist, as a sudden shift occurs and a patient may criticize the therapist on the grounds that the therapist has made the patient dependent and has become a self-aggrandizing and inept caretaker. Now, the patient is no longer weaker, being dependent on "good help," but stronger, and angry while defying "bad help." With a person who shifts into this hostile stance, it is hard for the therapist to point out that parts of the patient's self are in discord. The reason is that whatever the therapist chooses to say may be taken as an insult and repudiated. Withdrawal from the relationship punishes both the therapist, and the dependent part of self.

When a patient manifests a disturbed level of functioning, fluctuating into dissociation or fragmentation, for example, the goal of the therapist is to increase safety. This requires staying in some kind of perceptual contact with the patient, who may seem to be off in some other, unshared world, even though talking may continue. Hammering away at interpretations of a presumed, defensive withdrawal, in order to promote insight, is usually a mistake.

Time spent on restoring a working state is time well spent. And, spending time may be essential in working with disturbed-level patients. Perhaps by unconscious identification with the calm of the therapist, a patient may have the new experience of learning that even a tense conversation can continue onward. This is different from the patient's negative transference expectations.

Persons at a low-level type of personality functioning, as shown in Table 6.1, may be prone, under increased emotional stress, to enter states of mind in which their stream of thought is like a flow of sensations. In such patients the regressive states fail to include a parallel thinking channel of reflective self-awareness of determining the meaning of the sensory flow of conscious representations. A therapist's interpretation about what meaning is occurring in awareness, and communication, may fail to engage a patient's attention because the patient only hears the words and does not transform them into meanings.

At such moments, the therapist needs to engage in some other kind of discourse to maintain conversational connection. The conversational connection leads the patient, at least at a minimal level, to attend to the therapist rather than withdraw. Unconscious learning—by identification with the therapist's capacities for staying connected in communication—may begin to occur.

The therapist may join in the concrete sensation discourse, as in this dialogue:

Patient: (*punctuated with silences*) Light. I see it against dark. On the floor. From the window. Light streaming through the window. Just that.

Therapist: Do you have any idea why you notice that light pattern now, maybe avoiding your anger, which we were just discussing?

Patient:	(*stonily silent, averted gaze*)
Therapist:	I see the shadows between the panes of glass. The window wood blocks the light from outside. The light makes the rug look colorful.
Patient:	Yes. Light on the floor.
Therapist:	I understand it may have been difficult to discuss that topic we talked about a bit ago. Let's move our discussion to a different topic for now.
Patient:	OK. (*pause*) I did call my mother and…

Therapists may have to experiment with finding and communicating the kind of language that suits the patient's present-moment, information-processing capacities and degree of self-reflectivity. If and when an experiment fails, the therapist tries for any kind of give and take on a joint topic, focusing more on clarification than interpretation. This is in keeping with Alvarez (2010), who identified three levels of capacity for processing emotionality: the highest level is a patient able to think about feelings; a mid-level is a patient able to identify feelings but not think about them; and, in the lowest level of self-state functioning, the patient is not even able to access feelings as emotions, having just a stream-of-conscious sensations.

A patient may learn by imitating how the therapist amplifies a stream of sensations into words for feeling states, thus enabling the patient to get back to verbalized thinking and interactive conversations. Even so, patients at lower levels of personality functioning are so self-preoccupied that the clinician can feel shut out if he or she expects the conversational closeness usually experienced with patients at higher levels of personality functioning.

Complex childhood trauma and personality disorders

Childhood traumas, such as parental abuse, tend to lead to dissociative states at the time of trauma and, perhaps, to retroactive realization that a terrible betrayal of trust has occurred. Any severe and overwhelming event can impair identity formation or current self-organizational capacity, until it is mastered.

Recall of traumatic memories can be useful to the process of mastery, as reviewed in Horowitz (2011), see also Foa, Keane, and Friedman (2000). When mastered, trauma work can lead to identity growth. On the other hand, a vivid and quasi-relived perceptual kind of recall can further associate a memory with terror and lead toward identity degradations, a phenomenon called *retraumatization*. Retraumatization is more likely in patients with more disturbances in self-organization.

The therapist may aim to show a patient how to reflect on memories in a way that renders the trauma story as part of a past, not a harrowing retraumatization of re-experience. The roles of self and other in the childhood trauma are not a bizarrely-predicted, inevitable future. This means showing a patient how to examine a memory, even ones with intense sensory flashbacks, as a current narration, a version subject to flexible revision of attitude rather than a certainty as to what happened, a narration that can be revised to better understand cause-and-effect sequences and how the people involved were motivated at the time. Adult revision of a childhood story about a traumatic experience can build self-competence and reduce errors in self-blame (Herman, 2003).

Conclusion

The organizational level of self–other schematization defines the identity and relationship qualities of current personality functioning. Therapy can help people advance to higher levels of personality functioning. Different techniques for doing so depend on the accurate assessment of a patient's current level of functioning. The goal is experiential learning that can lead to more coherence in identity and to more constancy in intimate relationship capacities.

Chapter 7

Identity sense and personality disorders

Personality disorders are described in diagnostic manuals as persisting patterns of disturbance in identity and relationship functioning. In our discussions so far, we have emphasized these patterns in terms of self-states: the states of mind and the cycles of state fluctuation that, in persons with repetitive and maladaptive patterns, will lead to relationship conflicts and deficits. The disturbances summarized in Chapter 6 had to do with the properties of overall self-organization that might lead to patterns of harmonious state change, or highly maladaptive, explosive state changes. Generalizations were given in terms of levels of coherence in person schematic hierarchies. In this chapter, we will consider particular patterns as they are highlighted in the literature on typologies of personality disorder.

Before getting into these typological aspects of identity, I would like to repeat the point that, in clinical work, both the degree of coherence in self-organization, and the particular contents of persisting role-relationship models stored as schemas in the mind, are important. Making observations about form and content is often slow because the patient may only show some self-states in the comparative safety of the therapy situation, and only gradually describe the more disturbed occurrences that happen outside of it. That is why, for clinical utility, we need to personalize by making and revising the individual formulation of patterns, perhaps being guided by the study of various systems of case formulation that have shown reliability between clinicians, and predictive validity of pattern repetitions (Horowitz, 1997, 2005; Eells, 2010).

In order to share observations in the literature, some kind of typologies are necessary, because they allow searches to find the reports. Across diagnostic manuals, the DSM and the ICD as well as the PDM—and in the chapters of textbooks on personality disorder, as well as in the titles of books and journal articles—some typological headings have been found useful, especially in the education of clinicians. The most important of these were already discussed, in terms of identity disturbances, in Chapter 2. Now, we can reconsider some of the particular role and interaction scenario contents that might come up in treatment contexts.

Histrionic personality disorder

Histrionic personality disorder is known for theatricality, hence the term *histrionic*. The socially presented identity has characteristics that are selected from the person's propensities and then emphasized to gain attention. Within the conscious mind of the person, these social self-presentations may feel inauthentic, as if one is acting a role to give a false impression of what the self is actually hoping for in seeking a relationship.

The usual stereotype for histrionic personality disorder is a repeated and maladaptive self-presentation as very sexy, as if seeking an erotic love affair. In actuality, the person seeks a relationship in which the self receives good care and continued attentiveness from the other. What the person wants is constancy and closeness, not erotic mutuality. The self-presented social "identity" is not the same as the internal panoply of potential self-states. Other types of attention seeking may emphasize a different attractor if that suits the situation and nature of the person. A handicapped individual can seek attention with dependency needs and a gaunt person can present as if starving.

Typically, emotional states are variable depending on whether attention is received or withdrawn. A star-like and exhilarated self-state can fluctuate to become a state of intense despondency and sorrow. Self-beliefs of childish vulnerability and shame, or stronger revenging qualities may take center-stage. The person may activate role-relationship models that contain scenarios of revenging for grievances for others having found the self insufficiently attractive, revenge for having been used for pleasure, and then discarded.

With activation of a weak self-state, emotions feel intense and potentially so out of control that they are not self-owned. The person does not know, it may seem, what they are expressing, or why they are behaving in a way that is too theatrical to be authentic. Responsibility for relationship transactions is felt as if it belonged to the other person.

The person may not have words to cover the qualities of his or her emotional expression, appearing cloudy in conversations, as if without clear verbal representations. Felt emotions are based on whether or not one is in a state of being the center of attention. This may happen without conscious self-reflection—meaning, a conscious lack of recognition of one's own intentions—resulting in surprise at the sequence of events that do unfold, in response to the attractors used to get attention.

Self-awareness can improve as a result of the conversations about cause and effect, hope and fear, reality and fantasy, as they occur through the clarifications of therapy. The person learns to learn, finding ways for putting intentions, expectations, and feelings into words and requests of others.

The goal of therapy is to promote reflective self-awareness. Establishing the goal of seeking a more grounded sense of self, by putting together various parts of self, may be helpful. It may have been an intuitive aim that the person has never been able to articulate. Self-definition as an active agent of what happens, and as a regulator of emotion, can reduce the previous pattern of dissociative alterations between too-active and too-passive self-presentations to others.

Obsessive-compulsive disorder

An obsessive-compulsive personality typology defines the self primarily through work or productivity. Constricted experience, moralistic attitudes, and constrained expression of strong emotions prevail. Self-standards are typically very high and inflexible; perfectionism can interfere with achievement of realistic goals. Interpersonal relationships are impaired by difficulty in understanding others, and by the way others perceive the lack of cooperation that comes with the person's rigidity and stubbornness.

Emotions feel out of control in some of the usually compulsive person's self-states. For that reason, the person may ward off expression of feelings: the motive for this perhaps unconscious defensive operation, one that becomes all too habitual, is avoiding entry into a dreaded state in which the self feels out of control. An example of this might be entry into a self-state of being very angry, and then feeling one has harmed another with a behavioral expression of hostility, or that one has embarrassed oneself by seeming impulsive. Emotional expression limitations become such pervasive habits that the person annoys others with lack of warmth, spontaneous enjoyment, and authentic engagement. And such a person may appear to others to be much too punctilious, controlling, and perfectionistic.

Other people may experience the compulsive's contributions and actions in relationships as power struggles. This may include damage to the identities of partners and children. Controlling domineering, aggressive, and too-competitive upsurges, the person may ruminate about details, losing the big picture view of what is going on or what could go on in an interpersonal situation. What is done may be undone, redone, and retracted again: this compulsive behavior can be quite annoying to others. The person may feel remote from socially close affiliations and instead seek to connect with others through intellectual works, and achievements; when this driven behavior fails to garner sufficient success, deflations in self-esteem lead to depression, punctuated with anxious fearfulness at anticipating further failures in achievement.

The early steps in treatment to strengthen self-organization include confronting defensive generalizations such as intellectualization, undoing, and tangential thinking to avoid the emotional heart of important topics. Then, the repetitive interpersonal and maladaptive patterns of oscillating from too-superior to too-compliant can be identified in transference reactions. *Either-or* thinking, leaving out the important middle ground of roles for self and other is then clarified. New experiences can be explicated, showing self–other roles in a cooperating relationship, one of mutuality, empathy, and inter-dependence.

A relatively new relationship experience and a person schematic concept of cooperation is developed in the therapy alliance, as the patient gives up the binary extremes of either controlling the therapist's attention or feeling controlled by the therapist's suggestions, clarifications, and interpretations. This can occur without insight, though understanding the possibilities reflectively is helpful in enhancing the new kinds of conversation and negotiation. Interpretation of defensive avoidances of risking emotional closeness can help the person set aside the control operations and try out risky self-exposures. Identity definitions are expanded, in part, by identification with the therapist's stance of offering noncompetitive cooperation in explorations of meaning and emotion.

Avoidant personality disorder

Avoidant personality disorder is marked by intense self-criticism, low self-esteem, and fear of action. The result is usually a self-impairing reluctance to get involved in intimate relationships. The self-images of this prototype are of a diminished person: marginally competent in skills, weaker than experienced others, and defining himself as being inadequate without protective people or surroundings.

In therapy, the approach to maladaptive social strategies, like excessive avoidance of encounters, is to challenge the pattern. This usually creates stress, but the aim of potentially helping people to change for the better, in this way, often involves creating a state that could be called a "safe emergency." What is feared as an encounter outside of the therapist's office is offered *in* therapy. The patient is asked to assertively present a frank disclosure in an honest conversation about the matter with the therapist. Self-states of competence amidst risks may be learned as new experiences, leading to new self-schemas and role-relationship models.

The avoidant personality will go to extremes, including premature termination, to avoid even these "safe emergencies," though learning to endure them will gradually build a sense of stronger identity, through enhanced self-assertive abilities. The aim is for the patient to go from experiencing a sense of danger to a realization of safety in close encounters. This may be considered a new development of capacities for secure attachments.

Schizotypal disorder

Schizotypal personalities tend to be highly sensitive to proximity with others and they are too easily over-stimulated when relating to others through give-and-take conversations. Social situations are anticipated to undermine rather than enhance a secure sense of identity. Vulnerability increases when feeling dependent or falling in love. The self-state may shift to a sense of unwelcome merger with the identity of the other. Defensive withdrawal restores safety. A tolerable emotional distance is sought, and that can feel too remote for others, including helpers who usually want to engage more closely in open conversations. Emotional expressions in public are not congruent with context. Goals are often unrealistic or incoherent.

Relationships may be difficult to develop due to mistrust, anxiety, and a lack of understanding of others' motivations. The person's life story may suggest that he or she is not interested in forming relationships, but actually there is a deficit in social intelligence rather than a lack of interest. The person is motivated to be self-protective, preventing expected rejection, by focusing attention, values, and goals on self-oriented and self-controlled activities. That is why such an individual may exhibit detachment, a preference for being alone, and an excessive suspiciousness of others, including therapists.

Traits of social self-representation may include choices of odd and bizarre clothes, gestures, postures, verbalizations, and behaviors based on persistent but unusual beliefs about identity and the nature of attachments. Psychotherapy means learning about what a safe relationship might feel like, how it could be risked, and why it becomes worthy of maintenance.

Antisocial personality disorder

Antisocial personality disorder is marked by a lack of empathy and concern for the feelings of others as well as a lack of remorse after hurting others. Such individuals mainly relate to others by exploiting them and seeking power and pleasure for the self, without care, love, or trust for others. They do not value commonly held pro-social standards and may violate laws.

Their self-preoccupation does not include critical judgments about what effects they have had or may have on others, including weaker, younger, vulnerable persons, whom they exploit. They may charm and deceive the therapist, learning how to behave as if socially adapted, rather than learning new values and developing a self that is contained in role-relationship models of shared compassion and empathy.

Basic skills of relating are hard to teach in such situations. Identity theory does not help us much in this regard, except that some alliance may be achieved by proposing that the therapist's aim is to improve self-behaviors and self-skills in order to reduce patterns of self-injury. Counter-transference resentments over the lack of gratitude for expert help will need to be recognized and not acted out.

Borderline personality disorder

Borderline personality disorder sometimes presents explosive changes in states of mind, especially when the person is under certain types of perceived, high stress, as when the person feels about to be abandoned or feels that the self has been victimized. Within this typology, there are vulnerabilities to very impoverished, poorly developed, or unstable self-images, which can be so painful as to lead to self-harm or suicidality. Even in good times and stable relationships, the person is prone to enter self-states with extreme feelings of emptiness and a difficulty in regulating emotions.

Rage at the threats perceived, and misperceived, to the integrity of self can lead to hostile and under-modulated states of mind, including threats of harm to others. The shifts from good to bad states of viewing self and others manifest as interpersonal hypersensitivity. Unstable relationships result. People with this style may alternate between irrationally idealizing and devaluing a relationship, into "all good" or "all bad" versions. They may dissociate, split, and segregate memories of what was "all good" when things go "all bad."

The early aims of treatment are usually efforts at preventing the out-of-control states from destroying self, others, or the treatment opportunity. Directive teaching of how to recognize early warning signs, especially related to rage at others or self-disgust, and how to soothe the extreme edges of such feelings is very helpful. In the middle phases of treatment, using the language of identity and relationship theories is sometimes helpful in conveying hope and commitment to the slow but promising work of looking at feelings in the context of self and other transactions and expectations, with tactful but sometimes confrontational clarifications of projections within the immediate context of the therapeutic conversations.

Narcissistic personality disorder

Narcissistic personality disorder involves a disturbance in identity and interpersonal functioning. Its central feature is self-absorption. A less extreme splitting occurs: grandiose self-schemas are segregated from enfeebled or shameful self-schemas. These polar extremes are not harmonized by in between self-concepts, due to the absence of sufficiently developed superordinate schematization within self-organization. That is why drastic-appearing shifts in self-state may occur under stress, fluctuating between grandiose and deflated emotional experiences.

Seemingly independent and accomplished, such individuals are impaired because they are not truly connected with others in mutuality. They are covertly and excessively dependent on signs or fantasies of grandeur. They are often unaware of their own motives, and have difficulty recognizing the independent initiatives and needs of others. Their relationships may be used for personal gain, and a difficulty paying attention to others is often an obstacle to constancy and continuity.

In relationships with therapists, they need reflectance of their good attributes to maintain activation of the grandiose self-schemas and suppress the inferior self-schemas. A helpful remark may identify something to improve upon, but that may be taken as an accusation of weakness, and the person may enter a deflated self-state rather than learn beliefs that might lead to more supra-ordinate schemas, and more self-understanding, and better self-regulation. They may forge an idealizing transference, feeling great in the shadow of the remarkable helper, instead of learning how to give and take in the therapeutic conversations that can lead to real self-strengthening.

The narcissistic vulnerabilities found so starkly in the narcissistic personality disorder extend beyond its typological borders, as a category, and will be considered in the context of traits of pathological narcissism, in Chapter 8.

Chapter 8

Identity and self-esteem

A mature person has learned how to evaluate, respect, and treat himself kindly. This kind of self-esteem is healthy, and stands in contrast to the unhealthy aspects of pathological narcissism. Gaining such maturity of identity requires the kind of integration of self and relationship schemas suggested by the concepts of supra-ordinate person schemas. These integrative constellations of meanings pertaining to self and others advance functional capacities within the personality. Pathological narcissism involves more dichotomous thinking and binary attitudes than over-arching integration of attitudes. The pathology involves a habitual defensive position of quelling a dread of vulnerable self-isolation and inferiority by activating attitudes of irrational grandiosity, and schemas that use other people as mere extensions of the self.

Communities use status as carrots and social embarrassments as sticks. Children and adolescents are given mixed messages about these rewards. Modern cultures are fragmented, complex, and contain discordant blends of what is respected or stigmatized. Even within a family, parental figures may show discord and contradictions in key values. Adolescents, with emergent identities, may find it hard to maintain self-esteem through either self-submergence in group belonging or rebellious independence.

In many contemporary cultures, an individual has to learn to have a healthy self-esteem through self-appraisal in the midst of concerns for what others say about them, this requires personal evaluations about social performances such as meeting responsibilities. Along the way, low self-esteem is motivational, one wants to do better, but low self-esteem can lead to bitterness, fear, and sorrow, or to irrational compensatory maneuvers such as paranoid thinking or grandiosity.

Self-esteem is so important to social functioning and internal well being that a large amount of taxpayers' money was spent by the State of California during the 1980s to study it and provide legislators with a report. John Vasconcellos, the legislator who promoted the project, wrote in the Preface:

> I grew up in the 1930s in a constrained, traditional, Catholic family. I was educated in both public schools and Catholic (Jesuit) schools, through

college and law school. In school, I was a high-achiever, receiving awards and excellent grades. In adulthood, I became a prominent lawyer in a prestigious firm. My first campaign for a seat in the state legislature in 1966 was successful, and I have now been re-elected eleven times.

Yet, through it all, I had almost no sense of my self, no self-esteem. I worked for my successes only in a constant attempt to please others. My intellect functioned superbly, but the rest of my self barely functioned at all. I had been conditioned to know myself basically as a sinner, guilt ridden and ashamed, constantly beating my breast and professing my unworthiness. I had so little self-esteem that I lost my first election (running for eighth-grade president) by one vote—my own.

Awakening painfully to this problem, I began in 1966 to invest long and difficult years in redeveloping my self-esteem. My life and work have become increasingly focused on this compelling issue of self-esteem, not only in relation to my own development, but also in terms of enabling others to develop a strong sense of self.

(Vasconcellos, n.d., pp. xiv–xv)

Self-evaluations

Vasconcellos said that he had negative self-concepts conditioned in him by his upbringing. He felt he was a bad sinner, guilty, and ashamed, full of unworthiness. We can understand that he had self-schemas in his mind that functioned as critics, perhaps experiencing the criticism as if it were from representations of internalized or introjected others rather than himself. That is, his conscious thoughts and feelings may have been different, in terms of agent of origin of beliefs, from his stored, unconscious meaning structures, what we have been calling person schemas.

At times, Vasconcellos suggests he also consciously experienced a critic as a part of his self that was criticizing another part of him. At other times, in fluctuating states of mind, he may have experienced a chorus of internal self-talk as if from others, chastising him for sinning. He used psychotherapy to identify parts of self, and to develop higher levels of positive regard and self-integration. Worldly accomplishments alone, in spite of the glory achieved by being chosen by others to lead, had not sufficed to give him the peace of adequate self-esteem.

What, then, is self-esteem? Self-esteem is an outcome in which self-critics are proud of self-agency. The problem for most adults is maintaining self-esteem for a long period of time, before-during-and-after inevitable life crises, defeats, and losses. Values are very important components of this process, and internalized rules about what is right and what is even more right may conflict. Identity is, in part, a prioritized system of values, and appraisals of which rules were followed and which rules were broken, which goals were accomplished, and which goals were not met.

Value conflicts

The multiplicity of values presented by high levels of change in modern society leads to strain on traditional values, perhaps those learned without much conscious appraisal by self in the course of development. Basic principles, rising to consciousness as intuitions of right or moral behavior, compete for priority. In adulthood, the task of increasing self-coherence depends, in part, on reprioritizing these conflicting values (Levinson, 1977, 1996; Crain, 1985: Horowitz, 2009).

To repeat, in a post-modern stance, values are relative; they compete as contexts shift. Enduring self-esteem depends on sorting out these issues. Suitably complex values mediate modern, educated self-esteem.

Values are schematized, perhaps as person schemas such as role-relationship models that contain potential for the self-conscious emotional reactions, including pride, guilt, and shame. These potentials are activated and become conscious feelings when behaviors are compared with value standard. Acting in accordance with one's values furthers self-esteem, while acting against them decreases it.

People are motivated to avoid situations that could lead to embarrassment; they are also motivated to prepare for activities that can lead to glory. The person schematic scenarios used to organize plans for how to accomplish these goals change with maturation.

Winners and losers

A child recognizes who has many possessions and higher levels of power as well as the directions of social attention that define relative status. Most want "more success to be mine." As the person advances in maturity, he or she may reach the realization that success in life does not mean acquiring the most goods, having the most power, and always standing on a first-place podium.

These trophies, medals, or signposts do shore up self-esteem: self-esteem is also gained by appraising the amount of effort one has exerted to reach a goal. For example, a person who did his best to meet his own values can have high self-esteem even if social judgments did not categorize him as a victor. Pride can arise from having worked hard. Emotions such as shame and guilt can arise from a sense of not having tried hard enough.

This kind of positive self-esteem is also derived from acting with compassion, caring, accurate empathy, and maintaining responsibility in relationships. Loving promotes self-esteem, as does being loved. Caring gives self-esteem, and so does being cared for. Self-esteem is an appraisal of self-worth in affiliations with others. This is what psychoanalysts (Kohut, 1977; Erikson & Erikson, 1998; Solan, 1998) call healthy narcissism in contrast to pathological narcissism.

In healthy narcissism people develop a coherent sense of identity, maintain it over time in spite of many changes, and do so in a matrix of respect and caring trust. They maintain self-esteem as reflected, in part, by their recognition relationship to significant others. However, to others, a person's manifestations of self-estimation can seem too high, and the person may be called narcissistic. In Greek mythology,

Narcissus was so in love with himself that he gazed at his own reflection, loved his own beauty, and failed to take the opportunity to love Echo, a maiden who loved him. The popularity of this myth perpetuated a dichotomy, a falsely restrictive binary. What I mean by that is the assumption that a person is either totally self-centered or capable of loving and receiving love from others. Healthy narcissism contains both self-concern and caring-concern. The either selfish or loving categorizations are a false dichotomization. Pathological narcissism is different from this both self-caring and relationship-caring harmonization.

Pathological narcissism

In contrast to healthy kindness toward both self and others, pathological narcissism involves maladaptive self-preoccupation. Unlike normal self-interest and self-esteem, pathological narcissism leads to significant distortions in developing role-relationship models and so to repetitive impairments in relating to others. Externally, the public may see only the surface appearance of grandiosity and entitlement. Internally there is an attempt at self-consciousness based on an idealized view of self. Attention to accomplishments and social positions may be high. But inside the person also has a persisting vulnerability to activation of enfeebled self-states (Kohut, 1972). The person fluctuates between entitled pride and self-loathing, shame, and fear of social embarrassment. That is why the individual seems hypersensitive to perceived lack of empathy or support. A person may keenly apprehend what matters to another person, but instead of caring about the understood feelings, he or she may use that understanding to gain personal advantage.

A wish to feel grand, with self-appraisals as creative and skilled, may far exceed motives to cooperate with others, because the strength of ambition can cloak fears of weakness. A fear of being weakened, slighted, scorned, or embarrassed is excessive. In threatening situations, when someone might be at fault, blame may be externalized so the self is not at fault.

That is why a person with pathological narcissism overly attends to sources of either praise or blame in the interpersonal field (Kohut, 1972, 1977; Kernberg, 1975, 2009; Horowitz, 1981, 1989, 2009; Modell, 1984). Attention is severely biased toward people or environmental stimuli that might enhance self-esteem. As a corollary, negative acts of self may be omitted from memory and personal narrative, or else they can be distorted by rationalizations. Memories of events may be distorted, as meanings are slid around, to disassociate blame from self, as cause-and-effect sequences are examined.

When attributes of "who was who" in a transaction are reported, there is often a dislocation of traits between self and another person. Characteristics of the self that might seem foolish, weak, or inconsiderate are especially dislocated from the self and attributed to another person. It follows that the positive ideas, acts, or attributes of the other person are sometimes incorporated as if they had been actions of the self.

This inaccurate portrayal of personal attributes is not delusional, as in psychotic states. It involves subtle minimizations and exaggerations of meanings within the memory appraisal of a sequence of interpersonal events. The distortions of fact render a more positive self-image in a narrative structure of what happened.

The unfortunate results are a lack of true self-understanding, a defensive looking outward rather than an adaptive looking inward, and perhaps the person may seem to lie in reporting what actually happened. This is just one way that the pathological narcissist, by constantly externalizing blame, destroys relationship mutuality.

In order to stabilize self-states of only positive characteristics, plans may be made that are maladaptive. Choices that might involve recognizing that the self is not sufficiently skilled to embark on a course of action may be omitted from awareness. The individual may be quite alert to the emotionality of others while being opaque to their needs and desires, and as a result have trouble creating a relationship that is mutually facilitating and trustworthy. That is why the pathological narcissist appears to observers as if he or she forgives him or herself much too easily, and is lacking in forbearance in getting angry at others.

People with pathological narcissism fail in self-esteem because they repeat old patterns rather than learning from new opportunities for interpersonal understanding and closeness. Instead of repairing the inter-personal relationship problems that they have caused, they may fantasize illusory resolutions. Rather than accepting realistic limits, they may continue to pursue vain attempts toward perfection. Others see them as feeling excessively entitled.

Entitlement

In entitlement the person feels deserving of place, praise, and possession of the most resources. Any perceived talents are exaggerated to advance the excessive estimation of self. Tribute from others is expected, yet the narcissistic person may also underestimate the contributions of peers. Sometimes the ruthless thrust toward self-enhancement is concealed beneath pseudo-warmth. But the lack of concern for others is usually eventually recognized, perhaps leading to expulsion from institutional positions.

In due course, the other person learns he or she is being used, exploited, or is disliked. As that relationship is spoiled, the narcissist has to befriend a new acquaintance in an attempt to gratify his or her needs. Alternatively, the narcissist may bribe or blackmail the other to stay committed. In that case, it is common for the other to feel bored and restless, and loyalty is only feigned.

Shame

As life progresses, a pathologically narcissistic person becomes increasingly vulnerable to shame, panic, helplessness, or depression. With a loss of cohesiveness in the self-concept due to lapses in admiration and empathy from others, such persons may be vulnerable to entry into states of deflated self-esteem: they may even become self-destructive.

Feelings of envy, rage, paranoia, and outrageous demands on others often develop when a narcissistic person is subjected to the inner shame of degradation, as when experiencing the inevitable stress of aging. Such a person may interpret declining physical appearance and function as an intolerable embarrassment rather than an acceptable part of the shared human life cycle.

Charisma

Talented, wealthy, or exceptionally good-looking persons driven by narcissistic personality traits often display such charisma that they can continue to take on new relationships as old relationships fracture and perish. Social climbing is often a common feature, but the narcissist may also cling to acquaintances who can be relied upon to provide a positive reflection through flattery. And when the pathologically narcissistic person feels truly powerful, he or she may discard or depreciate persons who are no longer of use in bolstering his or her self-image.

Self-righteousness

Pathological narcissism carries a tendency to enter a self-righteous rage state of mind whenever blame is in the air (Kohut, 1972, 1977; Kernberg, 1975, 2009; Horowitz, 1981, 2012). Entry into a state of self-righteous rage may be quick and explosive. The trigger to this explosion is often the interpretation of an interpersonal encounter as involving some kind of insult to the propped-up grandiose self-state. The explosive state-change pattern is the observation that leads to classification of the person at lower levels of personality functioning, as discussed previously in Table 6.1.

Others often see the state of self-righteous rage as an exaggerated response because of the level of contempt that it contains. Whether manifested physically or verbally, the aggressive response exceeds the usual social standards of acceptable behavior. In spite of the socially unacceptable nature of the reaction, the subject feels justified in disparaging or even harming the other while in the self-righteous rage state.

This kind of towering rage state is pathological due to two important features. One is the inflated self-appraisal assumed during the state. This kind of grandiosity aims to defend against experiencing an inferior, bad, or damaged self-representation. The second feature in such rages is that others have to be blamed for what has happened. This is why the self-righteous state is sometimes called blind hatred. The person flying into such rages does not recognize that other persons have a right to exist, or that they have ever been good or kind to the self. There is a readiness to injure others on the grounds that they are at fault. A charismatic leader may even infect others with his attitude creating a mob-like state of scapegoating "inferior people" or "sub-human vermin."

Bitterness

Pathological narcissists may form a potential self-state of chronic embitterment, with an internal narrative in which the self is being unfairly abused by others or by fate. In this state, the person carries a chip on his or her shoulder and dares other people to knock it off. There may be belligerent demands for entitlement, angry confronting patterns or sullen-withdrawing forms of chronic embitterment.

Triangles in relationships of self-esteem

It useful to consider a triad of the self in relation to two others when it comes to describing some of the person schematic scenarios that lead to frequent oscillations between self-righteous and self-shamed states in pathological narcissism. The role of each party in such triangles can be prototypically viewed as hero, monster, and critic. The role of the critic is to admire the hero (ideally the self) and loathe the monster (usually a rival for someone's admiration). The use of the extreme label of "monster" is appropriate given that this person is often targeted with hostility as if they were sub-human.

An abundance of modern television shows and movies use the dramatic triangles of such monster and super-hero roles to permit highly destructive actions by the heroes, and members of the audience are the critics. If the hero is all-good (loves dogs, is nice to old people, smiles at children) and the monster is bad (kills animals, abuses elders, tortures children), critics (the audience) enjoy the cinematic violence as the hero climatically destroys the monster, amid applause and cheers.

Viewing others as monsters is a defense in which the human qualities of that person are forgotten while the supposed hero is in this self-righteous state. This defense allows the person to maintain the illusion that the critic is wholly admiring the self and utterly loathing the other as the monster. There can be no guilt, fear, or shame in this state as an abundance of hostility is permissible. The feeling of moral anger is an enjoyable energy, a thrill. It is only after transitioning from this state that the person may be aware of the possibility of shameful consequences of the destructive actions he committed during the state of rage.

Defensive operations

Grand self-schemas may ward off a tendency to activate states of mind organized by self-schemas of being weak, bad, damaged, or incomplete. These weaker attitudes tend to emerge in enfeebled self-states. The person then worries over identity, becomes obsessed with shame memories, and compulsive about achieving self-restorative operations, to others, the person may seem more anxiety-ridden. Extenders of self, self-enhancers, and others who are self-extensions may be sought out to defend against depressive and anxious experiences. As mentioned before, externalization of blame is another defensive operation aimed at protecting self-esteem.

Humiliation

Externalization of blame can amount to lying to others as well as the self. In an attempt to avoid acknowledging the painful reality, the person actually exacerbates the situation. The exposure of lying may lead to excruciating embarrassment, even suicidality. A person may also abuse stimulants in order neutralize painful emotions and through intoxication return to an illusory and grandiose self-state. The effect is transient, and social stigmatization may lead to the experiences the person attempted to avoid.

Personality growth

Pathological narcissism can be repaired, especially in the context of improved relationship strategies and experiences. Since blaming others may have been prominent in an individual's mental life for many years, clarification of what happened and who did what to whom will gradually lead to revisions of personal narratives. These new stories involve reappraisals of old attitudes as one reinterprets past memories. The goal is a more realistic view of the past, present, and the future.

As the person learns how to reconfigure self-organization in the direction of more reality and coherence, he or she becomes more empathic toward self and others, using newly acquired skills of reflective conscious awareness. Self-criticism gains a new, softer stance. This revision in self-judgment occurs in part through identification with others who are kinder and more caring than were early caretakers, or more consistently so. Prior care-giving figures may have been too harsh, unavailable, or unempathic, perhaps including parents who used the child as an extension of themselves rather than reflecting upon the child as a separate being. An empathic and constantly reliable therapist can provide new relational experiences.

In the context of psychotherapy or psychoanalysis, the critic position often waffles back and forth: what is within the patient is often regarded as if it is incipient in the therapist's mind. The patient wants to be idealized but expects criticisms. The patient tests the therapist to see what will happen. The therapist finds an "in between" safe position and manifests it. Then, by clarifications and interpretations, the therapist helps the patient find such evaluations within reflective self-awareness.

The therapist teaches how to attend to such potential evaluations of self and others, how to consider meanings, how to give them time, how to understand complex meanings rather than assigning self or other into abrupt and dichotomous categorizations. The goal of developing more supra-ordinate person schemas to contain expanded meanings can be described in everyday language appropriate to the patient's understanding. The patient has a pattern of categorizing some as great and some as inferior, under stress, someone is to blame and someone is not. The goal is looking for a range of meanings in between these polarities, and allowing for alternative role relationship appraisals. In expanding the understanding of situations and memories, defensive levels of exaggeration and minimization of the roles of self in cause-and-effect sequences are tactfully and gradually challenged.

This expansion of person schematic repertoires and cognitive processing capacities for appraising social information rests on safety in the therapy situation. In effect, less threat of degradation leads to defensive modifications. Early on, the patient has one kind of semantic structure for describing memories, later on an amplified semantic structure may be used to organize what is said.

For example, an early framework can be paraphrased as: "This bad thing happened. I was good and did xyz, they were bad and did rstuvw, and so they get the blame. You must agree with me." A later framework can be paraphrased as being organized by more in the way of supra-ordinate person schematizations:

> The context was abc. I planned to do defg and actually did, in interaction with them, hijk. They, meanwhile, did lmno and together we did pq, and then tried instead to rst. In retrospect, the consequences were bad because of blank blank blank. We would have been better if I had done uvw and they had done wxyz. So in the future I will consider uvwxyz. I accept my responsibility for hijk and will seek new opportunities with confidence from what I have learned.

This expanded way of organizing narratives and looking to the future is likely to be more successful than repeating pathologically narcissistic patterns.

Self-coherence increases as the person learns to accept more ambivalence in self-judgments as a normal part of mature adult life. Shame can become less menacing if it is gradually accepted as part of the human predicament rather than a catastrophic feeling that one's own soul is being murdered by the threats and avalanches of negative emotion. With maturation, some failures are to be expected as part of life. Faltering in competitions, economic loss, work failure, and relationship ruptures can be seen as blows to self-esteem that are unpleasant yet tolerable.

Conclusion

The development of supra-ordinate self-schemas fosters containment of embarrassing and idealized self-components. These organizations improve relationship capacities. Better relationships foster self-esteem. Self-esteem and pride-in-coping can sustain people through their most stressful phases of life.

Chapter 9

Identity change during mourning the loss of a loved one

They call loss of a loved one *heartbreak*; it can feel like part of the self is damaged. A sense of intact identity has to be reformed, based on new information about what the current loss of an attachment means to the self. Bereavement means a great deal of change: what the relationship meant, what consequences of loss will occur, and how the absence of an alliance affects all other interactions with the world. In this chapter, we will discuss just part of how and why that redefinition of self occurs, and examine it as a model of possible phases of identity growth. A short vignette illustrates how, during grief, intrusive self-states may occur early on, as altered, unexpected and unwanted experiences, before the change processes of grief work.

Mary

Mary's elderly mother died when Mary was middle-aged. Mary felt sorrowful, cried at the funeral, took a week away from her work and usual social activities, and then went through her mother's belongings, quietly contemplating memories as she decided what to keep and what to discard. This was hard emotional work and, when it seemed done, she resumed her life as usual. Weeks later, she was surprised to find herself preoccupied with unbidden images of hostile exchanges with her mother. She then found herself, episodically, to enter an unusual self-state of being hostile even to her amiable companions. She understood this as a kind of displacement of aggression that should more appropriately have been experienced as directed at her mother, but it still felt very strange, unlike her usual self, and a bit out of control.

During this phase of bereavement, Mary tried deliberately to recall her mother in the context of warm and empathic memories about their relationship. In trying, she found she could not conjure up any image at all of her mother's face, much less pleasant emotional ones. Instead, she intrusively pictured her own face, contorted with anger, as if seen in a ghastly mirror. This phase passed, with restoration of her ability to recall both positive and negative memories, but it also indicated an unexpected and intrusive encounter with some aspects of self.

Someone in the midst of grief can seldom accurately predict: *when* she might enter such a phase of having a particular mood, *what* memories of self as relating with the deceased would then be recalled, *when or if* strong emotions would be triggered by some reminder of the loss, or *why* a new attitude, perhaps of self-vulnerability, would emerge. In addition, few persons ever accurately predict the quality of anniversary reactions, yet most people have them. The unconscious mind tracks time and meanings that, in ways, go on as processes that are not directly reported to consciously reflective thinking. Strange changes in attitudes may surface as a certain date approaches.

Engel

The noted psychiatrist and psychoanalyst George Engel wrote of his anniversary reactions after his twin brother died suddenly from a heart attack, in the same way as their father had perished before him (Engel, 1975). His brother died at age 49; his father died at age 58. When Engel heard of the death, he felt stunned disbelief, and then began crying, 20 minutes later. Within a few hours, he was experiencing chest pains. Physicians discovered that Engel, too, had angina from coronary heart disease, though not an infarction. He expected that he, himself, would die quite soon.

When Engel reached 58, the age his father had been when he died, Engel made a number of unlikely errors in his conscious thought. He consciously thought of his father as dying at age 59 instead of age 58, though for many years Engel had feared that he, too, would die at 58. In this way he passed his fifty-eighth year without conscious anxiety, since the threat of his own death was projected forward as "not now" but maybe after his next birthday. After the threat had passed and he had survived his fifty-ninth birthday, Engel recalled that his father had, in fact, died at the age of 58. So, with his magical expectations, he was now beyond danger, even though he rationally knew better.

Such anniversary phenomena indicate how unconscious control processes can serve to reduce levels of fear and self-vulnerability. There is a balance between impulsive aims at mastery through processing the intrusive thoughts of a loss, and the unconscious, defensive aims to avoid emotional pain, perhaps to protect the self from unstable self-states. This varies over time, leading to phasic variation. We can consider the general patterns of phases of response in terms of degree of self-regression and self-redefinition, keeping in mind that no individual follows such phases like clockwork.

Grief pathology

In one of his most important theoretical papers, "Mourning and Melancholia," Freud (1917) examined the effects of the nature of the previous relationship with the deceased to predict whether normal or complicated grief would occur. He speculated that pre-existing ambivalence about the relationship predisposed the person to pathological forms of grief process. The bereaved person who experienced ambivalence toward the deceased before he or she died may translate that ambivalence, after the loss, into self-criticism, pitting one self-schema against another, unless that person has reached a harmonious level of self-organization. Grief pathology has since been explored in more complexity (Freud, 1917; Deutsch, 1937; Lindemann, 1944; Clayton, 1974; Glick et al., 1974; Pollock, 1978; Bowlby, 1980; Horowitz et al., 1984; Raphael, 1983; Osterweiss, Solomon, & Green, 1984; Windholz, Marmar, & Horowitz, 1985; Shear, Frank, Houck, & Reynolds,2005; Prigerson et al., 2012). Complicated or pathological grief has been noted to particularly prolong the multiple phases that may occur with normal, and more successfully completed grief (Prigerson et al., 2012).

Shear et al. (2005), Pollock (1978), Parkes (1964, 1972), Parkes and Weiss (1983), Freud (1917), and Lindemann (1944) have described the phases of grief in normal ranges of diverse bereavement reactions. I recently summarized these general phasic tendencies as: (1) an initial outcry of surprise and shock, perhaps including an urgency for searching to find and protect the lost person, however irrational, while also having possible regressive fears for the safety of the self; (2) denial and avoidance of reminders of the loss with a numb sense that the self need not change; (3) subsequent intrusive ideas and emotions which relate to the "we" with the other, as well as to the self as now "alone without the other"; and (4) a working-through phase that may include oscillating denial and intrusions as the person strains to resolve issues of anger, guilt, taking over functions of the lost relationship, and considering new relationship experiences. Then, a phase of relative completion may occur, perhaps with (5) redefinitional changes in identity (Horowitz, 2011).

The phase of outcry

Outcry contains a rapid assessment of the implications of the loss for the self. The sudden confrontation with bad news leads to a sharp rise in emotions such as fear, sadness, and anger. The appraisal that there is a sharp change between real events and expectancy schemas leads to alarm reactions associated with physiological changes in sympathetic, parasympathetic, and hormonal systems. The result may range from hyper-arousal to shock: the self feels differently, in a somatic sense.

A cascade of emotional experiences occurs during this early phase, as different implications of the death are considered. A person may form a working model in which the deceased is viewed as seriously harmed and critically in need of help. Because the deceased is modeled as harmed, the self is aroused to act, to reduce threat. As a result, the person may undertake frantic but hopeless activity to repair the hazardous condition. Some funeral rituals serve this obligation to "do something!" In addition, role reversals occur in person schematic models that become active working models: the self is depicted as attacked by the same possible causes of death. Ideas may occur like premonitions, "I cannot survive this!" or, "I shall somehow survive this," as well as appeals for divine help ("God help me!")

or expressions of rage ("God damn it!") or remorse ("I'm so sorry!"). Disavowal can also occur in the emotional exclamations that characterize this phase ("Oh no! It can't be! Say it isn't so!"). The sharp expression of emotional alarm may serve an evolutionary adaptive purpose. Sobbing may summon aid; shock and fear may elicit protection; remorse may cause renewed support; and rage may alert others to treat the self with tact and caution rather than demands.

The phase of denial

An individual is often aware that denial is operating, and is also aware of feeling numb or emotionally insulated. A conscious self-state may feel frozen, insulated, derealized, or depersonalized. A split-off, self-critical part may give self-talk, as in: "You didn't care very much, did you?" Or, the individual may be embarrassed that, because he or she didn't cry or express sorrow, others will think that he or she didn't care very much about the deceased.

Of course, some recognition of short-range consequences to the self is considered, but many other long-range effects are not contemplated. The use of schemas that model the deceased as if alive may be most prominent. This is reflected in statements such as, "*We* like to travel during vacations." A kind of dissociative "waiting for the return" may be felt.

The phase of intrusion

The denial phase may last for days, weeks, or even months. During this time, the mourner may have returned to many of the customary forms of his life. A sense of safety may be returning. Then, intrusive experiences increase in frequency and intensity.

Conscious recognition of the significance of a loss to the self becomes prominent during this phase. There is less use of inhibitions of salient topics as unconscious defensive operations to prevent intensely emotional self-states. Conscious efforts at inhibiting some trains of thought, however, may continue to curb the sharp pangs of emotion. This conscious, avoidance-type of attention control paradoxically contributes to the sense of intrusion when unwanted thoughts are represented.

During this phase, one may become preoccupied with an aspect of identification with the deceased in which one views oneself as vulnerable to death, as in Engel's report. One may experience the physical symptoms of the disease that killed the other, or in reveries strike magical bargains with the gods or spirit world to protect the self from the threat of death. One may feel guilty for worrying about dying when it is the other who died.

It is in this phase of grieving that a person may be helped by clarification and explanation of what is happening. The therapist can help to deepen understanding by giving small doses of interpretation of what is going on. The revised future of the self can be discussed as possibilities, separating realistic from fantastic appraisals.

The here-and-now working model of being alone differs from the enduring schema of expecting to be together. This discrepancy may motivate efforts to bring back the dead loved one, in fantasies and dreams. But the other is not there to reflect the self. Situations of being alone feel particularly empty and pangs of searing anguish may be felt. Eating a meal painfully emphasizes the absence of the previous support of identity though expected companionship.

Unanswered questions such as, "Who is to blame?" and "Why did this happen to me?" re-emerge during the intrusive phase. These themes may be organized by usually dormant self and relationship schemas, such as those wherein the self is viewed as bad and harmful to the other, or defective and somehow deliberately abandoned by the other. Survivor guilt, guilt over feelings of anger at the deceased, shame over feelings of helplessness, and fear of the future self-damage or death may recur as preoccupations.

The phase of working-through

Working through intrusive preoccupations carries the bereaved forward, toward a new kind of self-definition without the other as present in the world, though perhaps remaining very present in memory. Redefinition of self in past, present and future frames of reference occurs when time permits. Periods of equilibrium occur, in which neither defensive numbness nor emotional flooding is prominent. During this grief work, one reviews the story of the relationship with the deceased.

Self-reappraisals may occur in different and parallel channels of information processing. One channel may include weak, dependent, childlike self-concepts in relation to the deceased loved one as a parental figure, even when the real relationship was between peers. Another channel of information processing may include strong, dominating, or rivalrous views of self and other. The good and bad, clean and dirty, selfish and caring, and loving and hating themes will all have their time on the stage of reminiscence.

Decisions may now be made about how to redefine the self. The process of self-redefinition serves an evolutionary function. It prepares the person to take on new tasks, learn new skills, make new commitments after a loss, and harmonize various past narrations about the self. During this adaptive review of concepts, memories of the past self as contained in the relationship with the person who has been lost are reconsidered, and questions of what a new view of the present and future might be are examined. In the narration of the relationship story the elements are resorted to frame out what is now past, what is current, and what may now be expected of the future.

In this phase, the person may attempt a new relationship of the type that was lost. Another person is found to care for, relate to sexually, or to serve as a parental figure. Commonly, the new relationship is then colored by efforts to restore within it some aspects of the lost relationship. The discrepancy between the pre-existing role-relationship model with the deceased, and the different experiences occurring with the new person may lead to emotional responses. An alarm reaction of anxiety asks, in effect, why is this so different from what was expected? Patricia had various types of such alarms and serves as an illustration of processes of change in self-definition after a major loss.

Patricia

Before the murder of her young husband, James, Patricia was content in her roles as wife, mother, and professional. The loss was traumatic; she developed symptoms, and was variously treated with supportive psychotherapy, as well as anxiolytic and anti-depressant medications. She recovered control of her life, but two years later she sought a new kind of help because of her having a sense of having conflicting identities. She was no longer on medication or seeing the supportive psychotherapist.

The precursor to seeking this addition to her therapy was Patricia's embarking on a relationship with Sidney. Though Patricia desired to feel again like a vibrant woman, as deepening intimacy occurred, she had intrusive images of herself as if she were cheating on James, her deceased husband. She experienced tension and withdrew from Sidney.

Patricia compromised by stabilizing alternative self-states. In one, she felt herself to be a vulnerable woman, pining for her lost husband, and feeling incompetent without his customary guidance. In another, less problematic self-state, she felt cool and poised, a stoic and competent caretaker who managed home, children, and career. In this defensive self-state, she intended to be aloof from men in the future. That would relieve her from self-criticism and a sense of guilty cheating, if she gave in to loving again.

In therapy, this stoical stance was challenged. The therapist told her that she did not yet fully realize that James was really dead. "Your unconscious is the last to know such things," he said. He helped her to review the implications of all that had happened. She was able to express new concepts about herself, in both memories of the relationship with James, and new experiences and fantasies with Sidney. Patricia's in-therapy experiences included felt emotions about the therapist; relational attitudes organized by renewed activity of a pre-existing configuration of role-relationship models.

In this constellation of several role relationship models, each including somewhat different self-schemas, there were wishes to depend on the therapist for guidance, as she had her husband and her father before marrying her husband. But these wishes for guidance were connected to another, more dreaded part of the dependency configuration. In this more feared role-relationship model she appraised herself as being a too-dependent girl and the consequences were self-criticisms that lowered her self-esteem and led to depressive ideas of having a limited future. Patricia did not want to continue being so dependent on a man in her life for guidance on every impending decision.

Work in therapy clarified how she shifted between two polar two self-states in dichotomous thinking: the shifts were back and forth between: (1) her need to be very dependent on a man, and (2) she did not need a man at all, she was autonomous. She was able to reflect on these either-or attitudes and conceptualize possible relationship attitudes in between. With increased boldness she empowered the belief that, as an aspect of her total identity as a woman, she was now again capable of love and experiencing mutuality on an equal footing, neither subservient nor domineering.

Patricia was able to see that her future self-definitions could be different from her past and present self-definitions. She could be supported in her independence rather than losing her personal autonomy. If she experienced self-competence in close verbal encounters with the therapist, she could experience it in close verbal and physical encounters with Sidney. She would not be cheating on James, and she would not become as dependent on Sidney as she had been dependent on James. She could go forward and seek happiness without shame at being too dependent or guilt that she was cheating on James.

Patricia re-schematized her relationship roles with her deceased husband and her new self-definitions. She re-schematized James as beyond dying: as safely dead, and no longer expecting her fidelity. She re-schematized herself as a mature adult rather than late adolescent: she was older, wiser, and more capable than when she had accepted James' proposal with the urging of her father to do so. With Sidney, she would be mutually giving and receiving.

She liked her new self-definition as a woman of many parts: career woman and mother, mature daughter caring for older parents who were becoming a bit disabled, and as an intimate partner in loving a man. In the course of a prolonged and complicated grieving process, she had done much to reduce sorrow, fear, and remorse about the past. Now, in terms of identity growth, she had reduced contradictions between her roles and developed a stronger sense of being continuously her revised self in a realistically possible future. She felt a firm sense of pride for having gone through a very difficult life passage.

Completion

Completion marks the relative end of mourning. It is "relative" because some mourning and continuing revisions of identity persist beyond a period called bereavement. Anne provides an example.

Anne

Anne attended a talk I gave on the relation of unconscious factors leading to the phenomenology of grief experiences. At the coffee break, she told me that, just that morning she had finally put on earrings left to her by her mother upon her death, two years before. Up until the day of the talk, she had left them untouched in her jewelry box. She had attached no significance to the act that morning, but during the talk she realized she had decided—unconsciously—to symbolically complete her mourning by claiming the earrings as her own. Anne also thought that she had probably signed up for the conference for this reason.

Level of personality functioning and mourning

Pre-existing personality disturbances may be accentuated during grief, but completion of mourning may lead to personality growth. The bereaved person's sense of self-coherence can be hampered during grief by: (1) the absence of past self-reflection previously received in connection with the person now lost; (2) the tendency to feel damaged by unmet dependency needs; (3) unresolved ambivalence leading to anger at abandonment, and guilt for hostile thoughts, perhaps based on magical expectations that prior hostile wishes made the death happen; (4) concepts that the loss is an ordained punishment of the self; and (5) pre-loss disturbances in how well supra-ordinate self-schemas configured together the person's multiple self-schemas and role-relationship models. All these developmentally conflictual themes, if present, can be worked-through. Post-grief personality growth can especially involve increased harmonization and development of supra-ordinate self-organization.

Conclusion

The human species has evolved with a capacity for mourning that reaches its fullest expression in a mature adult. Even so, most people take a long time for grief work in order to reach a point of relative completion. Part of that process leads to growth in a sense of identity: harmonized self-concepts that are up-to-date and a self-evaluation as a person ready to plan and experience a future life.

Lines of research on self-organization

Assessment of levels of identity coherence and relationship functioning can be accomplished using systematic interviews and scales for *observer reports*, as well as simpler and more expedient *self-report scales*. In addition, one can undertake narrative analyses for self and relationship concepts using methods for intensive *reviews of recorded interviews*, and/or transcripts of such interviews. These observer, self-report, and narrative analytic methods will be discussed in sequence.

Observer methods

The task of clinically evaluating a patient's level of personality functioning can be focused on estimating the level of self and relational schematization, and using that level as a quantitative measure. Obtaining enough information by structured interviewing is required and those who make the inferences require training if reliability is to be achieved. The expense in research is justified because we are dealing with complex judgments and the data achieved so far will have strong predictive validity: they predict the course of symptoms after assessment, and they predict the relation of techniques used by therapists to eventual outcome (Horowitz, Marmar, Weiss, DeWitt, & Rosenbaum, 1984; Piper, Azim, Joyce, & McCallum, 1991a; Høglend et al., 2006; Gamache et al., 2009; Diener & Monroe, 2011; Mullin & Hilsenroth, 2012).

An interesting two-polarities model led to an Object Relations Inventory (ORI) and some significant research findings (Luyten & Blatt, 2013). The polarities are: (1) interpersonal relatedness, as an emphasis on attachments within personality structure; and (2) an emphasis in the minds of subjects on self-definitional issues. Of course, a well-balanced personality structure means attention to both identity and to relationships, the two in balance and in harmony. However, the two-polarities model suggests that unhealthy personality functioning might be an over-emphasis on either one, as in self-definitional preoccupations, as was discussed in Chapter 8 as pathological narcissism, or on relational insecurity as discussed in Chapters 3 and 4.

The Object Relation Inventory (Blatt, Auerbach, & Levy, 1997) yields a subscale that represents the clinician's inference of levels of self–other differentiation. As used by Bers, Besser, Blatt, and Harpaz-Rotem (2013), the subscale ranges on 10 levels from low (lack of differentiation) to high (reflectively constructed and integrated representation of self and other in reciprocal and mutual relationships). The field uses similar psychoanalytic theoretical constructs across different frames for clinician interviews and subsequent judgments.

A conceptually related scale is called the Structured Interview for Personality Organization (STIPO). The STIPO is an observer-interviewer-based scale based on psychoanalytic theory of identity, object relations, and pathological defenses (Caligor, Clarkin, & Kernberg, 2007). The clinician scores his or her inferences about a subject on scales of identity, object relations, primitive defenses, reality testing, moral values, and aggression. On factor analyses, these scales overlap, are highly correlated, and are not clearly differentiated. Identity stands out as an important correlate of all scales and object relations plus primitive defenses are next. These three constructs are emphasized in the categorization outline of levels of disturbance found in Table A.1, which is a repetition of Table 6.1.

The two-polarities model and the STIPO cover concepts embedded in work on OLSOS (Organizational Level of Self and Other Schematization) (Horowitz et al., 1984; Horowitz, 1991). The emphasis in all of these models on identity,

Table A.1 Levels of integration of self–other schematization

Level	Description
Harmonious	Internal desires, needs, frustrations, impulses, choices, and values are appraised as "of the self." Realistic pros and cons are examined to reach choices of rational action and restraint. Grounded in self, one views others as separate people with their own intentions, expectations, and emotional reactions. Perspectives on relationships approximate social realities. Past and present views of self and relationships are integrated, allowing a sense of constancy and modification of ambivalence. State transitions are smooth, appropriate, and adroit. Warm and caring relationships are maintained over time in spite of episodic frustrations. Emotional governance prevents out-of-control states.
Mildly conflicted	While good-enough relationships are formed, in his or her closest work and intimate affiliations the person displays states that contain varied intentions, manifesting as conflicting approach and distancing tendencies. On examination, these alternations are based on fluctuating attitudes about self in the relationship. Most commonly, fears of rejection may limit warm and caring attachments to others or fears of subordination limit high levels of cooperation. The person appraises self with a variety of critical judgments, some too harsh, some too lax. State transitions occur between positive and negative moods but the shifts in state are remembered and not explosive surprises or emergence of alternative selves.

(Continued)

Table A.1   (Continued)

Level	Description
Vulnerable	A sense of self-regard deteriorates under stress, criticism, and increased pressures to perform. To protect from feelings of inferiority or enfeeblement, grandiose supports of self-esteem may be utilized. Concern for the well-being of others may be considered less important than using others as tools for self-enhancement. Surprising shifts from vigor and boldness to states of apathy, boredom, or unpleasant restlessness may occur. Because of insufficient self-organization, the person may shift between being loving and suddenly, overly demanding and suddenly appeasing. Emotional governance is reduced and undermodulated rage may erupt at others who are perceived as insulting and blamed for otherwise shameful deflations in self-esteem.
Disturbed	Life seems organized by using various self-states and some of them seem like a break with reality. Errors in self–other attribution occur. Undesirable self-attributes and emotions are projected from self to other. The actions of self may be confused in memory in terms of who did or felt what and shifts in self-state may be accompanied by apparent forgetting of what happened in the alternative state of mind. Memories frequently combine fantasies with once-real elements. State transitions can be explosive. Dissociative identity experiences re-occur under stress and forgetting and then remembering may occur in segregated states of mind and views of self.
Fragmented	A massive chaos of selfhood can occur and, as a counter to cope with the high distress, the person frequently feels aroused to high defensiveness and accusation of others, as if under attack. As a needed repair of damage to self, the individual may regard self as merged with another person. Or the person may withdraw in a hibernated, frozen, self-protecting coping effort that appears bizarre and self-damaging to others. Parts of the bodily self may be infused with the "badness" and disowned from self-images. This sense of chaos is very painful and can give rise to poorly regulated emotional impulses, including potentially suicidal or homicidal urges, intensified because the strange behaviors lead to social stigmatization.

relationship, and those defenses that are conspicuously irrational because they distort self–other attitudes has influenced the levels of personality functioning design developed by one sub-group for diagnostic use in DSM-5 (Bender, Morey, & Skodol, 2011). Skodol and colleagues (2011) and Zimmerman et al. (2012), suggested that *self-identity functioning* in personality evaluation should be seen as related to two categories: identity, and self-direction. The domain of *interpersonal function* was also divided into two capacities: empathy and intimacy (the details are available in DSM-5, Section III, for future research considerations, see American Psychiatric Association, 2013, p. 781).

The format I prefer is of course from work by my colleagues and I when forming the Organizational Level of Self and Other Scale, a set of complex potential observations reduced to a five-point judgment by a clinician who asks about current self-state and past relationship stories, even in a challenging way to increase the exposure of attitudes. That is, the observer seeks a dimension from harmony to fragmentation of attitudes in terms of the issues summarized in Table A.1.They select the level with a number between 0 (high level of harmonization of person schemas) to 4 (most disturbed level of organizing schemas). This reduction of a very complex set of inferences has the advantage that it yields a single score for the stratification of subject samples, and this single number can serve as a subject clustering variable or, for an individual, an evaluation of change over time, perhaps in an extended psychotherapy or analysis.

The information in Table A.1 can be used to develop structured interviews, asking particular questions. My colleagues and I use a format that asks clinicians to observe interview behaviors for the issues summarized in Table A.2. The five issues are attention focusing capacity, reality appraisal capacity, capacity to control emotional self-states, capacity to stabilize a sense of identity, and capacity to adhere over time to personal goals/values. The observer considers a range

Table A.2 Level of personality functioning (as an extension for mental status examinations)

Ask questions that suit each category: see following page for suggestions. From what you observe and infer, circle a single score for each category from 0–4 with 4 as the most disturbed level.

Capacity to Focus Attention versus Distractibility
Score 0 1 2 3 4

0 = Shifts focus when asked to and stays on topic	*4 = Wanders off topic and does not return to it*

Capacity to Accurately Appraise Reality versus Magical Thinking
Score 0 1 2 3 4

0 = Can make and clarify appraisals and differentiate illusory sensations from perceptions	*4 = Confuses fantasies with perceptions*

Capacity to Control Emotional State versus Dysregulation of Emotionality
Score 0 1 2 3 4

0 = Communicates feelings and their causes in well-modulated states	*4 = Communicates feelings with inappropriate intensity and frequency*

Capacity to Maintain Sense of Identity versus Shifting Self-States
Score 0 1 2 3 4

0 = Has a coherent sense of selfhood	*4 = Dissociates self-states or depersonalizes*

Behavior Reflects Good Judgment versus Impulsive Behavior
Score 0 1 2 3 4

0 = Adheres to self-owned rules, values, and priorities	*4 = Actions are disorganized and sudden, rules are broken*

(Continued)

Table A.2 (Continued)

The observations leading to the above scores are from interviews that may have stressful topics, such as the mental status examination and questions about suicidality and violence potential as well as recent crises. Additional questions to possibly ask in the interview are from the self and relational disturbances cluster of the BITSR (Brief Interview for Traumatic Stress Responses; Horowitz, Shumway, and Fields, in process). The subject is asked by the interviewer if they agree or disagree with certain statements, and if they agree to say a bit more. These questions may also be stressful and can lead to a change in mental state, leading to the observations for the five scores above.

- Lose your temper
- Don't know why you are angry
- Have intentionally done yourself physical harm
- Think constantly about sex
- Don't like sex
- Take risks that could cause trouble for you
- Ignore signs of danger
- Feel that you are living in a dream, or see your life before your eyes as if it were a movie
- Know that your friends consider you to be impulsive
- Feel that you have done something wrong
- Worry that certain people will take unfair advantage of you
- Feel that most people can't be trusted
- Shift back and forth between strong love and strong hate
- In close relationships, you are hurt again and again
- Feel a sense of worthlessness or hopelessness
- Expect the worst
- Feel that life has no meaning

between polarities anchored in Table A.2, yielding scores between 0 and 4, with 4 as high disturbance in personality functioning. Structured clinical interviews provide observers with particular questions, as in the BITSR (Brief Interview for Traumatic Stress Responses) method under development by Horowitz, Shumway, and Fields, for complex PTSD. In the session, as part of the evaluation, the clinician may ask whether the subject agrees with the statements shown as bullets (second page of Table A.2). These statements are stressful probes which may evoke signs of disturbance, the signs that can help the clinician make complex observational patterns that can lead to ratings as shown in Table A.2.

A typical problem in this line of clinical research is the halo effect of knowing the subject's symptoms. At worst, this halo effect can become circular: patients seen as having more symptoms are then inferred to be more disturbed in level of schematic organization (Klug & Huber, 2009). Nonetheless, reliability and predictive validity suggest that observer inference-type assessment can be useful. For example, consider a study comparing Borderline Personality Disorder (BPD) patients with Major Depressive Disorder (MDD), and normal controls with

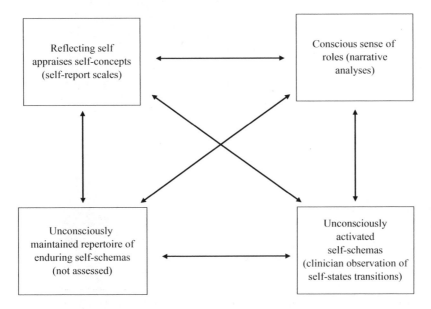

Figure A.1 Interaction of levels of awareness on self-identity (and relevant types of assessment)

a group of patients with only MDD. Observer inferences on self-coherence of the subjects showed that they judged the BPD patients with MDD to have more inconsistency in their sense of self-coherence than the contrast group of patients with only MDD, or the control group (Klug & Huber, 2009).

Self-report methods

Self-report scales usually depend upon the availability of a reflecting self-appraisal, as the perceiver, thinker, and planner of personal experience. These are conscious derivatives of a self-state and involve a self-interpreter reflecting on self-representations as shown in Figure A.1. Variations in self-state, while important in assessing coherence of identity and levels of functioning of self-organization, are often neglected in self-report methods because the variation is often not fully consciously recognized and easily reportable.

Higgins (1987) developed a model that did relate to multiple self-states in that his model could predict emotional vulnerability stemming from the contradictions between several selves: an actual self, an ideal self of personal values, an ought-to-be self that one felt a duty to be because of others, and a can-do self. In empirical studies, Higgins found that a large discrepancy between an actual and ideal self was related to symptoms of depression. An actual and ought-to-be discrepancy was related to symptoms of anxiety (Avants, Margolin, & Singer, 1993; Strauman & Higgins, 1987).

Kihlstrom and Cantor (1994) found that different self-concepts, and hence possibly self-state variation, emerged when narratives involved priming of meanings with different relationships: self-concepts of being with one's mother were different from self-concepts associated with ties to one's father. Some configurations of supra-ordinate self-schemas may be found in narrative analysis and seem specific to certain types of relationships, such as leader–follower, husband–wife and parent–child (Hart, Stinson, Field, Ewert, & Horowitz, 1995).

The CPI (California Psychological Inventory) has a measure related to *self-coherence.* Scores on self-coherence predicted symptom course over years (Gough, 1957, Block, 1961; Antonovsky, 1979). More recently, self-reports for the centrality to a core identity of traumatic experiences have been developed (Berntsen & Rubin, 2006, 2007). Childhood trauma has been found much more frequently in personality disorders, leading to the concept of complex combinations of self–other attitudes and vulnerability to later traumatization. On such a scale, more reports of trauma affecting identity predicts as well, as may seem obvious, more negative affectivity.

Other investigators have found that consistency of authenticity of self-feelings in different states predicted both physical and psychological well-being. These effects operated as statistically independent predictors from the Big-Five Personality Traits (Sheldon, Ryan, Rawsthorne, & Hardi, 1997; Wood, Linley, Maltby, Baliousis, & Joseph, 2008). People who manifest consistency in reported traits of self had higher levels of reported self-esteem (Diehl, Jacobs, & Hastings, 2006).

Tedeschi and Calhoun (1996) used the Post Traumatic Growth Inventory (PTGI) as a self-report measure of identity that was experienced as changing after a dire life event. The self-report has many items, perhaps making it too time-consuming for subjects filling out packets of self-report scales. Fewer items were used by Campbell et al. (1996). Their self-report measure had 12 items endorsed on 5-point Likert scales, yielding one total score related to felt self-coherence. These items are a surrogate for self-coherence and had high internal consistency (a =. 85). My colleagues and I developed, independently and in parallel, a shorter 5-item self-report measure that takes just a minute or two to complete and that can be used easily as a repeatable measure (Horowitz, Sonneborn, Sugahara, & Maercker, 1996).

The items in our *Self Regard Questionnaire (SRQ)* are shown in Figure A.2. These items are endorsements on a Likert scale and the five items add to a single score of self-regard: the higher the score, the higher is estimated self-coherence. It has been found to be predictive of health or distress over time in two studies.

In one of these studies, the SRQ was filled out by 53 HIV-positive gay men. Blood tests assessed their CD4+ cell counts (a measure of immune functioning) initially and again two years later. Greater self-regard at baseline was significantly and positively correlated with higher CD4+ counts 29 months later, and this association was strongest among persons with less concealment of their gay identity (Ulrich, Lutgendorf, Stapleton, & Horowitz, 2004). Concealment of one's sexual identity can be stressful due to discord between inner self-concepts and social self-presentation. Great and continuing discords can lead to identity disturbance experiences (Ulrich et al., 2004).

Please circle one number for each question indicating your average over the last week.

Sense of my facial appearance	1 2 3 4 5 6 7 8 9 10 Least attractive I can really look Most attractive I can really look
Sense of fatigue	1 2 3 4 5 6 7 8 9 10 Least rested I can really get Most rested I can really get
Sense of healthy body	1 2 3 4 5 6 7 8 9 10 Least healthy my body can feel Most healthy my body can feel
Sense of healthy mind	1 2 3 4 5 6 7 8 9 10 Least healthy my mind can feel Most healthy my mind can feel
Sense of my identity as a whole person	1 2 3 4 5 6 7 8 9 10 Least sense of myself as a whole person Most sense of myself as a whole person

Scoring: Add up all the items for a single sense-of-self-regard score.

Figure A.2 Self-regard questionnaire

Source: Horowitz et al. (1998).

In a second study, the Self-Regard Questionnaire in the latter study predicted subsequent symptoms of distress in widows. Bereaved men and women filled out a battery of scales including the SRQ six months after the death of their spouse. The scores on the Self-Regard Questionnaire at six months were inversely correlated with their symptom level scores on the Beck Depression Inventory at 14 months ($r = 0.49$, n = 74, $p < 0.001$). These scores were correlated with various measures taken at 6 months as shown in Table A.3 (Horowitz et al., 1996).

In sum, very brief self-reports such as the SRQ serve as surrogates for complex issues of level of self-coherence when observer methods are too expensive to use. Such scales of very few items can produce repeated measures that can

Table A.3 Self-regard questionnaire (SRQ) scores*: correlations with other measures six months after death of a spouse (n = 78)

	r	p
Impact of Event Scale	−0.55	<0.05
Beck Depression Inventory	−0.58	<0.05
Beck Anxiety Inventory	−0.53	<0.05
Social Desirability (Marlow, Crown)	−0.03	NS

Source: Horowitz, Sonneborn et al. (1996).

Note: * Scores on the SRQ averaged at 32 out of a possible maximum of 50.

allow assessment of identity disturbance levels in large populations over time. These data can be used in epidemiological surveys, longitudinal developmental studies, and as predictors of both process and outcome in psychotherapy research studies.

Stating core self–other attitudes through structured analyses of narratives

Analysis of psychotherapy or other narratives can provide a rich perspective on the degree of conflictual identity versus identity coherence as well as the meaningful contents of self-concepts. For example, research on change in narrative qualities, studied by analysis of what patients say, has shown a positive correlation with symptom improvement of these related constructs: more coherence, more mental rather than external contents, and more self-reflection on such contents over time in therapy (Gonçalves & Machado, 1999). In a series of studies, Pennebaker and colleagues (1999) found that the construction of a narrative about previous traumatic events was related to improvement, using quantitative context-analytic methods, in accord with my own findings (Horowitz et al., 1993).

One can proceed in steps to reduce the complexity of information. Grounded Theory methodology (Strauss & Corbin, 1990) has led to a method for finding and refining useful categories. Configurational analysis offers pre-determined categories (Horowitz, 1991). Highlighting or annotating sections of transcripts identifies the specific views on identity and relationships. Categories of self-attribution can be defined if repetitions of what the person says about himself or herself occur. Summarizing these as paraphrases is a form of qualitative analysis. Counting repetitions within abstracted categories, using other judges, leads to quantitative analyses.

Using blind judges can lead to reliability studies, if and when the expense of doing that is warranted. Transaction sequences are then identified and may involve a reordering of spoken sequences. Imagined elements (e.g. I thought I had become a ghost) are designated as such to differentiate them from features found in stories about what really happened in the past (e.g. I woke up from a fainting spell in the hospital).

It may help to use a mapping sentence: "subject" does toward "object," "object" does toward "subject." The sentence used for paraphrasing can be amplified for roles: "I, who am like this and that, did thus and so, to my husband, who is like this and that, and he responded by doing thus and so, and I then felt like this." The later "and then I" can identify acts of self-appraisal leading to shame and guilt or pride and self-esteem.

One can take discourse and paraphrase it by such formats in order to clarify the key descriptions either of *self*, *other*, or *we*. This locates repetitions, which are then summarized. In collaborative research with colleagues, a format for summarization has been useful. We called the format a role-relationship model (RRM) (Horowitz, 1988, 1991, 1998, 2005; Horowitz & Eells, 1993; Hart, Stinson, Field, Ewert, & Horowitz, 1995). We summarized the desired, dreaded, and compromised or defensive role-relationship model versions into a role-relationship model configuration (RRMC). These contained multiple selves in each of the RRMs of an RRMC. Self-organizational coherence concepts would be a new judgment involving the level of discord and contradiction between repeated self-concepts.

In alternative methods, computer-assisted counts of adjectives, adverbs, and verbs where "I" is the subject can also be utilized. Such methods often draw out values and value conflicts, which are frequently important in post-traumatic identity growth phenomena. These have cultural, ethnic, and ethnographic extensions, as suggested in Chapter 4.

Example of narrative analysis

The following is an example of a categorical mapping sequence: "subject" does toward "object," "object" does toward "subject." The sentence used for paraphrasing can be amplified for roles: "I, who am like this and that, did thus and so, to (other person), who is like this and that, and he responded by doing thus and so, and I then felt like this." One can take discourse and paraphrase it by such formats in order to clarify the key descriptions. This locates repetitions, which are then summarized in RRMs. The RRMs that are repeated and related to a specific relationship or type of attachment or role are then assembled into configurations of role-relationship models.

Here is an example of using a mapping sentence to paraphrase what is said. Jane says:

> went for a weekend with Joe and it started out to be happy and exciting for me. Just when I wanted to enjoy how good I looked for the first time in a long time and what a fine man my new boyfriend really is, I suddenly thought of my previous husband, Andy, who died a year ago. I felt, I don't know why, it seems so irrational, very, very bad, like I was a cheater even though Andy and I are divorced.

The paraphrase begins with the "I, who am," format like this: "I who am a cheater, felt badly about Andy." By implication, one might add that she views Andy as accusing her of cheating. The paraphrase also has: "I, who am a good-looking woman, was happy and excited with Joe, who is a fine man." The latter can go into a *desired* RRM, the former "cheater" into a *dreaded* RRM. An approach-avoidance dilemma results in the cycle or sequence. It could be paraphrased as:

> (Whenever) I, who am a good-looking woman, wanted to feel happy and excited with Joe, who is a fine man, I, who was faithful to Andy, felt badly that I am cheating on Andy.

As a result of activating this role-relationship model of loving Joe and so hurting Andy, she enters a guilty-feeling state of mind. The roles of the two men in this kind of dilemma are also reversible. Jane feels guilty toward Joe if she retains her identity as faithful to and intimate with only Andy. In this way, a recurring identity and roles of relationship conflict can be clarified. The narrative analysis could go on to explicate social values within this subject as rules for right conduct, i.e., whether or not a marriage is permanent even after divorce.

Values in narratives

Values can define particular attitudes used in the self-judgments, and expected social judgments. RRM and RRMC formats can be used to depict desired and dreaded or "defensively safe" roles and repeated practices to conform to norms within a social group. Self-defining beliefs may be in harmony or in conflict with the assigned roles and beliefs of ethnic peers (Agar, 1986). An individual rejecting a social role of unquestioning reverence to a parent, for example, might expect criticism from all others in the social group, even if there are others who also do not hold that belief. The values can be stated in words, and these words paraphrased for clarity.

Values can be assessed as self-critic schemas depending on culture, and these may act within the theater of the mind as if the values were from deities, spirits, or pluralities of "we" as in "my people" (Shweder, 1991). Narrative analysis can also be used in evaluating attachment styles in adults and in familial settings (Hesse, Cassidy, & Shaver, 2008).

Subjectivity in narrative analyses

We who see science as a sober and objective search for the truth also recognize that subjectivity can be either an obstacle or an advantage. Such subjectivity is a liability when researchers have personal biases. An analysis of our own subjectivity for its liabilities should be included when defining the categories or thematic structure used in narrative analysis. Bias can operate in the categories used to organize narrative analyses, even though categories for judgments by those who examine the narratives improve the chances for objectivity and relative truth. In addition, the people being studied have their inevitable subjective biases and we want to include those in our analysis of their narratives.

In the type of narrative analysis discussed, subjectivity is sometimes an aid. The method of configurational analysis promotes paraphrasing of what the speaker of the narrative meant (Horowitz, 1991, 2005). It includes intuitive recognition of patterns of omission, and may fill in some of the missing information with inferences about defensive avoidances and what was likely avoided. This controlled subjectivity of the judge can enrich validity. Looking for reliability in inferences across judges can reduce the danger of subjective bias. Judges can be asked to independently review the same narratives, using the same categories, but be blind to the other judge's reports.

Usually it is expedient to use single judges, however, my colleagues and I have found that discussions and teamwork can clarify patterns and reach agreements by consensus. For example, two research teams can read and infer the patterns of contents in a defined set of narratives. A third team does not infer patterns, but rather is charged with examining the reports of the two teams for degrees of agreement and disagreement. This can even add a quantitative component, a type of reliability rating. This can also lead to qualitative re-examination of differences in contents reported by the two analytic teams (Horowitz et al., 1984; Horowitz, Eells, Singer, et al., 1995).

Conclusion

For large group studies I suggest that researchers use surrogate self-report variables centered on negative identity experiences for repeated measures. In smaller groups, a clinician-based score is desirable and I suggest investigators ask interviewers to pay attention to a patient's variability in self-states, in a range from smooth to explosive transitions in a subject's apparent mood states, as a way of arriving at categories of self-coherence, as shown in Table A.1. I suggest that narrative analysis is most useful as an intensive research method that can lead to ever better theory-formation and generation of hypotheses as well as a way to derive newer items for self-endorsement or clinician inference.

Glossary

Belief structure   The associational pattern that connects elements of information into a meaningful complex.

Character   Learned, enduring, and only slowly changing meanings that lend continuity over time to a sense of identity and constancy in attachments.

Configuration   A set of associatively related beliefs. Harmonious configurations have well-integrated elements. Conflictual configurations have poorly integrated elements and identity disturbances may be associated with them.

Configurational analysis   A system of formulation that describes: (1) the phenomena to be explained; (2) states in which the phenomena do and do not occur; (3) themes that lead to state changes and defensive controls used to regulate emotions of these themes; and (4) configurations of self–other attitudes.

Cycles   Repeated sequential patterns of states.

Declarative knowledge   Beliefs that can be consciously represented and communicated.

Defensive control processes   Mental activities, often operating unconsciously, that ward off dreaded states (e.g., anxiety, terror, rage, depression). These regulatory processes make use of the inhibitions and facilitations that can affect both form and content of thought as well as the schemas used to organize thinking, feeling, planning, and acting.

Identity   Awareness of the self as a continuous and, usually, coherent entity that perceives, thinks, feels, decides, and acts. Conscious identity rests upon the belief structures of unconscious self-organization.

Insight   A realization about the cause and/or effect of a situation or the connection between elements in a pattern.

Integrated attention   The result of putting together or blending of meaning that allows a person to navigate easily between various modes of representation, for example, translating visual images into words.

Magical thinking   Arriving at assumptions based on fantasy rather than realistic appraisals of situations.

Motives   A term referring to the reasons for decisions. There may be motives to enact as well as motives to restrain action or even conscious representation of impulses. Motives usually refer to enduring themes and the word *intention* is used to refer to more transient aims.

Parallel processing   The simultaneous processing of information in relatively separate channels. For example, a person might appraise a current danger situation and plan intentions by emotional cognitive processing organized by: (1) a competent self-schema as well as by (2) an incompetent self-schema. The parallel processing can yield divergent conclusions.

Personality   An individual's enduring and slowly changing sets of beliefs, preferences, values, traits, and tendencies that make up a unique and time-continuing pattern of moods, thoughts, and behaviors. Personality consists of the important components of identity and relationship patterns, and capacities for emotional regulation.

Person schema   A person schema is regarded as an organized whole including body images, traits, roles, values, and mannerisms. The subordinate parts are beliefs nesting in a hierarchy leading up to the whole.

Preconscious processing   Preparatory mental manipulation of information that occurs before conscious representations. Parallel processing may proceed using different role-relationship models as organizers of information.

Procedural knowledge   "Know-how" that can lead to automatic action sequences without the concomitant "declaration" of such knowledge in reflective consciousness, operating preconsciously or unconsciously.

Projection   A defensive operation in which an attribute of self is externalized and regarded as if coming from or motivating another person.

Psychodynamic configuration   A constellation of motives, defined at the psychological level, in terms of wishes, fears, and defensive strategies. A configuration of conflict usually involves a wishfully impulsive aim, a threat that is viewed as a possible consequence of impulsive action toward a desired goal, and a defensive posture that, though compromising the wish, avoids the feared consequences.

Reflective consciousness   A state in which self-observation is incorporated in awareness or sensory streams.

Relational model   A descriptive, generalized, cognitive map of the roles, transactions, aims, and sense of connection between self and others.

Representations   Iconic or symbolically encoded meanings that are capable of either conscious awareness or communicative expression. Representations occur in modes such as images, lexical (verbal) propositions, or enactive (somatic) propositions.

Reschematization   The process of altering belief structures by adding new elements, reorganizing prior elements, and altering linkage strength patterns in the associational connection between elements. The result can modify personality-based attitudes and assumptions.

Role-relationship models (RRMs)   Inner schemas and scripts blueprinting interpersonal transactions as well as attributes of self and others. Some RRMs are *desired*: they depict positive outcomes that a person seeks to achieve. Others are *dreaded*: they depict negative outcomes that a person seeks to avoid. Some RRMs are compromises to avoid wish-fear dilemmas. Of these, some are *problematic compromises*, containing symptom-causing elements, and others are *protective compromises*, containing coping or defensive elements.

Schema   A usually unconscious meaning form that can serve as an organizer in the formation of thought. Schemas influence how motives reach awareness and action. Schemas tend to endure and change slowly as the integration of new understanding modifies earlier forms. Small-order schemas can be nested into hierarchies acting as larger-order or supra-ordinate schemas.

Self-concept   The term self-concept can refer to a recurrent belief of self-attribution that can be (and at least once has been) consciously represented.

Self-confidence   An endowing and slowly changing trait of having trust in one's own abilities and qualities that is usually considered as a range from high to low. If one has a pattern of labile shifts in self-states, as from competent to incompetent, the end result may be unnerving lapses in self-confidence.

Self-esteem   An overall evaluation of self as a worthwhile human being who is entitled to exist. Such self-appraisal may range from high to low. If one has fluctuating self-states, then one's self-esteem may be unstable.

Self-objects   Other people or things that an individual views as an extension of him/herself rather than a fully separate and autonomous person.

Self-organization   A person's overall set of available schemas and supra-ordinate schemas.

Self-schema   An unconscious organizer of many features of the individual into a holistic pattern. The term self-schema can apply to enduring codifications that, when activated, influence patterns of thought, mood; and behavior. This pattern, when experienced, is a self-state.

Self-state   A temporary constellation of self-feelings and definitions of identity that is due to activation of self-schemas as the current organizer of connections between sets of information, interacting with current sensory inputs, including how the self is perceived as being reflected by significant others.

States of mind   Combinations of conscious and unconscious experiences, with patterns of behavior that can last for a period of time and that can be observed by others as having emotional, regulatory, and motivational qualities.

Supra-ordinate self-schema   A larger structure that contains a configuration of multiple more subordinate self-schemas.

Theme   A theme is usually large, complicated, and composed of varied topics. Narrative themes can represent complex patterns in a relationship and a sense of personal past stories and future destiny.

Therapeutic alliance   The relationship that forms between a patient and a therapist, which allows them to work together toward a mutual goal.

Transference   The displacement of ideas, feelings, motives, and actions associated with a previous relationship to a current relationship to a degree that the belief structure is, in part, inappropriate. A therapist's *counter-transference* classically involves reactive feelings elicited by the patient's transference toward the therapist. However, commonly, clinicians use counter-transference to refer to the feelings of the therapist toward the patient, regardless of whether or not those feelings are brought on by the patient's transference or by the therapist's own transference toward the patient.

Working model The currently active schematic organization of beliefs. A working model usually combines perceived information with information from activated, enduring schemas.

Bibliography and further reading

Agar, M. H. (1986). *Speaking of ethnography*. Beverly Hills, CA: Sage.

Ainsworth, M. (1973). The development of infant–mother attachment. In B. Caldwell, & H. Ricciute (Eds.), *Review of child development research*. Chicago: University of Chicago Press.

Ainsworth, M., Blehar, E., Waters, E., & Wall, S. (1978). *Patterns of attachment: A psychological study of the strange situation*. New York, NY: Basic Books.

Alvarez, A. (2010). Levels of analytic work and levels of pathology: The work of calibration. *International Journal of Psychoanalysis, 91*, 859–878.

American Psychiatric Association. (2013). *Diagnostic and statistical manual of mental disorders* (5th ed.). Arlington, VA: American Psychiatric Publishing.

Amlo, S., Bogwald, K. P., Heyerdahl, O., Høglend, P., Marble, A., Sjaastad, M. C., & Sorbye, O. (2006). Analysis of the patient-therapist relationship in dynamic psychotherapy: An experimental study of transference interpretations. *American Journal of Psychiatry, 163*, 1739–1746.

Amodio, D. A., & Frith, C. D. (2006). Meetings of minds: The medial frontal cortex and social cognition. *Nature Reviews Neuroscience, 7*, 268–277.

Antonovsky, A. (1979). Health, stress, and coping. *Archives of General Psychiatry, 41*, 438–448.

Avants, S. K., Margolin, A., & Singer, J. L. (1993). Psychological interventions and research in the oncology setting: An integrative framework. *Psychotherapy: Theory, Research, Practice, Training, 30*, 1–10.

Azim, H. F., Piper, W. E., Segal, P. M., Nixon, G. W. H., & Duncan, S. C. (1991). The quality of object relations scale. *Journal of Personality Assessment, 73*, 449–471.

Baars, B. J. (1986). *The cognitive revolution in psychology*. New York, NY: Guilford Press.

Baldwin, M. (1992). Relational schemas and the processing of social information. *Psychological Bulletin, 112*, 461–484.

Barnes, H., & Parry, J. (2004). Renegotiating identity and relationships: Men and women's adjustment to retirement. *Ageing and Society, 24(02)*, 213–233. Available at: http://dx.doi.org/10.1017/S0144686X0300148X.

Baumeister, R. F. (1998). The self. In D. T. Gilbert, S. T. Fiske, & G. Lindzey (Eds.), *The handbook of social psychology* (Vol. 2, 4th ed., pp. 680–740). New York, NY: Oxford University Press.

Beck, A. T. (1967). *Depression: Causes and treatment*. Philadelphia: University of Pennsylvania Press.

Beck, A. T. (1976). *Cognitive therapy and the emotional disorders.* New York, NY: International Universities Press.

Beck, A. T. (1987). Cognitive models of depression. *Journal of Cognitive Psychotherapy: An International Quarterly, 1,* 5–37.

Bender, D. S., Morey, L. C., & Skodol, A. E. (2011). Toward a model for assessing level of personality functioning in DSM-5, Part I: A review of theory and methods. *Journal of Personality Assessment, 93(4),* 332–346.

Benjamin, L. S. (1974). Structural analysis of social behavior. *Psychological Review, 81,* 392–425.

Benjamin, L. S. (2003). *Interpersonal reconstructive therapy.* New York, NY: Guilford Press.

Berlin, H. A. (2011). The neural basis of the dynamic unconscious. *Neuropsychoanalysis, 13,* 1.

Berntsen, D., & Rubin, D. C. (2006). The Centrality of Event Scale: A measure of integrating a trauma into one's identity and its relation to post-traumatic stress disorder symptoms. *Behaviour Research and Therapy, 44,* 219–231.

Berntsen, D., & Rubin, D. C. (2007). When a trauma becomes a key to identity: Enhanced integration of trauma memories predicts posttraumatic stress disorder symptoms. *Applied Cognitive Psychology, 21,* 417–431.

Bers, S. A., Besser, A., Blatt, S. J., & Harpaz-Rotem, I. (2013). An empirical exploration of the dynamics of anorexia nervosa: Representations of self, mother, and father. *Psychoanalytical Psychology, 30(2),* 188–209.

Bion, W. R. (1957). Differentiation of the psychotic from the non-psychotic personalities. In E. B. Spillius (Ed.), *Melanie Klein today: Developments in theory and practice.* Vol. 1: *Mainly theory.* London: Routledge.

Bion, W. R. (1997). *Taming wild thoughts.* London: Karnac Books.

Blatt, S. J., Auerbach, J. S., & Levy, K. N. (1997). Mental representations in personality development, psychopathology, and the therapeutic process. *Review of General Psychology, 1,* 351–374.

Blatt, S. J., & Luyten, P. (2009). A structural–developmental psychodynamic approach to psychopathology: Two polarities of experience across the life span. *Development and Psychopathology, 21 (03),* 793–814.

Block, J. (1961). Ego identity, role variability, and adjustment. *Journal of Consulting Psychology, 25,* 392–397.

Blos, P. (1941). *The adolescent personality: A study of individual behavior.* New York, NY: Appleton-Century Company.

Blos, P. (1979). *The adolescent passage.* New York, NY: International Universities Press.

Bowen, M. (1978). *Family therapy in clinical practice.* Northvale, NJ: Jason Aronson Inc.

Bowlby, J. (1969). *Attachment and loss,* vol. 1: *Attachment.* New York, NY: Basic Books.

Bowlby, J. (1973). *Separation: Anxiety and anger.* New York, NY: Basic Books.

Bowlby, J. (1988). *A secure base: Parent–child attachment and healthy human development.* New York, NY: Basic Books.

Bretherton, I., & Waters, E. (1985). Attachment theory: Retrospect and prospect. *Monographs of the Society for Research in Child Development, 50(1/2),* 3–35.

Brody, G. H., Moore, K., & Glei, D. (1994). Family processes during adolescence as predictors of parent–young adult attitude similarity: A six-year longitudinal analysis. *Family Relations, 43(4),* 369–373.

Bromberg, P. M. (2003). Something wicked this way comes: Trauma, dissociation, and conflict: the space where psychoanalysis, cognitive science, and neuroscience overlap. *Psychoanalytic Psychology, 20,* 558–574.

Bronfenbrenner, U. (1979). *The ecology of human development: Experiments by nature and design*. Cambridge, MA: Harvard University Press.

Bucci, W. (1997). *Psychoanalysis and cognitive science: A multiple code theory*. New York, NY: Guilford Press.

Butler, J. (1990). *Gender trouble: Feminism and the subversion of identity*. New York: Routledge.

Campbell, J. D., Trapnell, P. D., Heine, S. J., Katz, I. M., Lavallee, L. F., & Lehman, D. R. (1996). Self-concept clarity: Measurement, personality correlates and cultural boundaries. *Journal of Personality and Social Psychology, 70(141)*, 141–156.

Cass, V. C. (1979). Homosexual identity formation: A theoretical model. *Journal of Homosexuality, 4*, 219–235.

Clarkin, J. F., Yeomans, F. E., & Kernberg, O. F. (2006). *Psychotherapy for borderline personality: Focusing on object relations*. Arlington, VA: American Psychiatric Publishers.

Cloninger, C. F. (2004). *Feeling good: The science of well-being*. New York, NY: Oxford University Press.

Cloninger, C. R., Svrakic, N. M., & Svrakic, D. M. (1997). Role of personality self-organization in development of mental order and disorder. *Development and Psychopathology, 9*, 881–906.

Coleman, E. (1982). Developmental stages of the coming out process: Homosexuality and psychotherapy. *Journal of Homosexuality, 7*, 31–43.

Craig, A. D. (2004). Human feelings: Why are some more aware than others? *Trends in Cognitive Science, 8*, 239–241.

Craig, A. D. (2008). Interoception and emotion: A neuroanatomical perspective. In M. Lewis, J. M. Haviland-Jones, & L. Feldman-Barrett (Eds.), *Handbook of emotions* (pp. 272–288). New York, NY: Guilford Press.

D'Argembeau, A., Jedidi, H., Balteau, E., Bahri, M., Phillips, C., & Salmon, E. (2012). Valuing one's self: Medial prefrontal involvement in epistemic and emotive investments in self-views. *Cerebral Cortex, 22(3)*, 659–667.

Dawkins, R. (1989). *The selfish gene*. Oxford: Oxford University Press.

Dell, P., & O'Neil, J. (2009) *Dissociation and the dissociative disorders: DSM-V and beyond*. New York, NY: Routledge.

Demascio, A. (2010). *Self comes to mind*. New York, NY: Pantheon.

Diehl, M., Jacobs, L. M., & Hasting, C. T. (2006). Temporal stability and authenticity of self-representations in adulthood. *Journal of Adult Development, 13(1)*, 10–22. Doi:10.1007/s10804-9001-4.

Diener, M. J., & Monroe, J. M. (2011). The relationship between adult attachment style and therapeutic alliance in individual psychotherapy: A meta-analytic review. *Psychotherapy: Theory, Research, Practice, Training, 48(3)*, 237–248. Doi:10.1037/a0022425.

Diguer, L., Pelletier, S., Hebert, E., Descoteaux, J., Rousseau, J-P., & Daoust, J-P. (2004). Personality organizations, psychiatric severity and self and object representations. *Psychoanalytic Psychology, 21*, 259–275.

Drapeau, M., & Perry, C. (2004). Childhood trauma and adult interpersonal functioning: A study using the Core Conflictual Relationship Theme Method (CCRT). *Child Abuse and Neglect, 28(10)*, 1049–1066.

Eells, T. D. (2007). *Handbook of psychotherapy case formulation* (2nd ed.). New York, NY: Guilford Press.

Eells, T. D., Horowitz, M. J., Singer, J. L., Salovey, P., Daigle, D., & Turvey, C. (1995). The Role-Relationship Model method: A comparison of independently derived case formulations. *Psychotherapy Research, 5*, 161–175.

Ellenberger, H. F. (1970). *Discovery of the unconscious: The history and evolution of dynamic psychiatry*. New York, NY: Basic Books.

Emde, R. N. (1988). Development terminable and interminable. I. Innate and motivational factors from infancy. *International Journal of Psychoanalysis, 69,* 23–42.

Erikson, E. H. (1950). *Childhood and society*. New York, NY: W.W. Norton.

Erikson, E. H. (1959). *Identity and the life cycle*. New York, NY: International Universities Press.

Erikson, E. H. (1968). *Identity, youth, and crisis*. New York, NY: W.W. Norton.

Erikson, E. H. (1970). Reflections on the dissent of contemporary youth. *International Journal of Psychoanalysis, 51(1),* 11–22.

Erikson, E. H., & Erikson, J. M. (1998). *The life cycle completed*. New York, NY: W.W. Norton.

Fairbairn, W. R. D. (1954). *An object relations theory of the personality*. New York, NY: Basic Books.

Falkenbach, D. M., Howe, J. R., & Falki, M. (2013). Using self-esteem to disaggregate psychopathy, narcissism, and aggression. *Personality and Individual Differences*. Doi:10.1016/j.paid.2012.12.017.

Feldman, M. (2007). Addressing parts of the self. *International Journal of Psychoanalysis, 88(Part 2),* 371–386.

Field, N. P., Hart, D., & Horowitz, M. J. (1996). The content of self-and other-concepts: A network perspective. *Imagination, Cognition, and Personality, 16(4),* 357–378.

Foa, E. B., Keane, T. M., Friedman, M. J., & Cohen, J. A. (2009). *Effective treatments for PTSD: Practice guidelines from the International Society for Traumatic Stress Studies*. New York, NY: Guilford Press.

Fonagy, P. (2001). *Attachment theory and psychoanalysis*. London: The Other Press.

Fonagy, P., Gyorgy, G., Jurist, E., & Target, M. (2000). *Affect regulation, mentalization, and the development of the self*. London: The Other Press.

Fonagy, P., Roth, A., & Higgit, A. (2005). Psychodynamic psychotherapies: Evidence-based practice and clinical wisdom. *Bulletin of the Menninger Clinic, 69(1),* 1–58.

Fonagy, P., Steele, M., & Steele, H. (1998). Reflective functioning manual for application to the Adult Attachment Interview, version 5. Available at: http://mentalizacion.com.ar/images/notas/Reflective%20Functioning%20Manual.pdf.

Fonagy, P., & Target, M. (1997) Attachment and reflective function: Their role in self-organization. *Development and Psychopathology, 9(4),* 679–700.

Freud, S. (1910). Infantile sexuality and neuroses. *Standard Edition* (vol. 11, pp. 40–48). London: Tavistock.

Freud, S. (1950). *The interpretation of dreams*. New York, NY: Modern Library.

Fromm, E. (2006). *The art of loving*. New York, NY: Harper Perennial Modern Classics.

Gabbard, G. O., & Horowitz, M. J. (2010). Using media to teach how not to do psycho-therapy. *Academic Psychiatry, 34,* 27–30.

Gabbard, J. A., Hales, R. E., & Yudofsky, S. C. (2008). *Textbook of psychiatry* (5th ed.). Arlington, VA: American Psychiatric Publishing.

Gamache, D., Laverdiere, O., Diguer, L., Hebert, E., Larochelle, S., & Descoteaus, J. (2009). The Personality Organization Diagnostic Form: Development of a revised version. *The Journal of Nervous and Mental Disease, 197,* 368–376.

Gardner, D. G., & Pierce, J. L. (2011). A question of false self-esteem: Organization-based self-esteem and narcissism in organizational contexts. *Journal of Managerial Psychology, 26(8),* 682–699. Doi:10.1108/02683941111181770.

Gatersleben, B., Murtagh, N., & Abrahamse, W. (2012). Values, identity and pro-environmental behaviour. *Contemporary Social Science: Journal of the Academy of Social Sciences*. Available at: http://epubs.surrey.ac.uk/719548/.

Goffman, E. (1961). *Asylums: Essays on the social situation of mental patients and other inmates*. New York, NY: Anchor Books.

Goffman, E. (1974). *Frame analysis*. New York: Harper.

Gogtay, N., Giedd, J. N., Lusk, L., Hayashi, K. M., Greenstein, D., Vaituzis, A. C., Nugent, T. F. 3rd, Herman, D. H., Clasen, L. S., Toga, A. W., Rapoport, J. L., & Thompson, P. M. (2004). Dynamic mapping of human cortical development during childhood through early adulthood. *Proceedings of National Academy of Science, USA, 101(21)*, 8174–8179.

Goldberg II, H. M., & Malach, R. (2006). When the brain loses its self: Prefrontal inactivation during sensorimotor processing. *Neuron, 50*, 329–339.

Gough, H. G. (1957). *The California psychological inventory*. Palo Alto, CA: Consulting Psychology.

Grotstein, J. (1981). Who is the dreamer who dreams the dream and who is the dreamer who understands it? In J. Grotstein (Ed.), *Do I dare disturb the universe? A memorial to Wilfred R. Bion*. Beverly Hills, CA: Caesura Press.

Gruber, J., Harvey, A. G., & Purcell, A. L. (2011). What goes up can come down? A preliminary investigation of emotion reactivity and emotion recovery in bipolar disorder. *Journal of Affective Disorders, 133*, 457–466.

Gunderson, J. G., & Sabo, A. N. (1993). The phenomenological and conceptual interface between borderline personality disorder and PTSD. *American Journal of Psychiatry, 150*, 19–27.

Hart, D., Stinson, C., Field, N., Ewert, M., & Horowitz, M. (1995). A semantic space approach to representations of self and other in pathological grief: A case study. *Psychological Science, 6(2)*, 96–100.

Harter, S. (Ed.). (2012). *The construction of the self: Developmental and sociocultural foundations* (2nd ed.). New York, NY: Guilford Press.

Herek, G. M. (2009). Hate crimes and stigma-related experiences among sexual minority adults in the United States: Prevalence estimates from a national probability sample. *Journal of Interpersonal Violence, 24*, 54–74.

Herman, D. (2003). *Narrative theory and the cognitive sciences*. Stanford, CA: CSLI Publications.

Herman, J. L. (1997). *Trauma and recovery*. New York, NY: Basic Books.

Hesse, E., Cassidy, J., & Shaver, P. R. (2008). The Adult Attachment Interview: Protocol, method of analysis, and empirical studies. In J. Cassidy, & P. R. Shaver (Eds.), *Handbook of attachment: Theory, research, and clinical applications* (2nd ed., pp. 552–598). New York, NY: Guilford Press.

Higgins, E. T. (1987). Self-discrepancy: A theory relating self and affect. *Psychological Review, 94(3)*, 319–340.

Higgins, E. T. (1997). Beyond pleasure and pain. *American Psychologist, 52*, 1280–1300.

Hochschild, A. R. (2012). *Outsourced self: Intimate life in market times*. New York, NY: Metropolitan Books/Henry Huet & Co.

Horowitz, M. J. (1981). Self righteous rage and the attribution of blame. *Archives of General Psychiatry, 38*, 1233–1238.

Horowitz, M. J. (1987). *States of mind: Configurational analysis of individual personality* (2nd ed.). New York, NY: Plenum Press.

Horowitz, M. J. (1988). *Introduction to psychodynamics: A new synthesis.* New York, NY: Basic Books.

Horowitz, M. J. (1990). A model of mourning: Change in schemas of self and other. *Journal of the American Psychoanalytics Association, 38(2),* 297–324.

Horowitz, M. J. (1991). *Person schemas and maladaptive interpersonal patterns.* Chicago: University of Chicago Press.

Horowitz, M. J. (1998). *Cognitive psychodynamics: From conflict to character.* New York, NY: John Wiley & Sons.

Horowitz, M. J. (2005). *Understanding psychotherapy change: A practical guide to configurational analysis.* Washington, DC: American Psychological Association.

Horowitz, M. J. (2009). Clinical phenomenology of narcissistic pathology. *Psychiatric Annals, 39,* 124–128.

Horowitz, M. J. (2011). *Stress response syndromes* (5th ed.). Northvale, NJ: Jason Aronson.

Horowitz, M. J. (2012). Prototypical formulation of pathological narcissism. In J. Ogrodniczuk (Ed.), *Treating pathological narcissism.* Washington, DC: American Psychological Association Press.

Horowitz, M. J. (2013). Disturbed personality functioning and psychotherapy technique. *Psychotherapy, 50,* 438–442.

Horowitz, M. J. (2014). Grieving: The role of self representation. *Psychodynamic Psychiatry, 42,* 89–98.

Horowitz, M. J., & Arthur, R. J. (1988). Narcissistic rage in leaders: The intersection of individual dynamics and group process. *International Journal of Social Psychiatry, 34,* 135–141.

Horowitz, M. J., & Eells, T. (1993). Role relationship model configurations: A method of psychotherapy case formulation. *Psychotherapy Research, 3,* 57–68.

Horowitz, M. J., & Eells, T. (2006). Configurational analysis: States of mind, person schemas and the control of ideas and affect. In T. Eells (Ed.), *Handbook of Psychotherapy Case Formulation.* New York, NY: Guilford Press.

Horowitz, M. J., Eells, T., Singer, J., & Salovey, P. (1995). Role-relationship models for case formulation. *Archives of General Psychiatry, 52(8),* 625–633.

Horowitz, M. J., & Lerner, U. (2010). Treatment of histrionic personality disorder. In J. F. Clarkin, P. Fonagy, & G. O. Gabbard (Eds.), *Psychodynamic psychotherapy for personality disorders: A clinical handbook* (pp. 289–310). Washington, DC: American Psychiatric Publishing.

Horowitz, M. J., Marmar, C., Weiss, D. S., DeWitt, K. N., & Rosenbaum, R. (1984). Brief psychotherapy of bereavement reactions: The relationship of process to outcome. *Archives of General Psychiatry, 41(5),* 438–448.

Horowitz, M. J., Sonneborn, D., Sugahara, C., & Maercker, A. (1996). Self regard: A new measure. *American Journal of Psychiatry, 153,* 382–385.

Horowitz, M. J., Stinson, C. H., Fridhandler, B., Ewert, M., Milbrath, C., & Redington, D. (1993). Pathological grief: An intensive case study. *Psychiatry, 56,* 356–374.

Horvath, S., & Morf, C. C. (2010). To be grandiose or not to be worthless: Different routes to self-enhancement for narcissism and self-esteem. *Journal of Research in Personality, 44(5),* 585–592. Doi:10.1016/j.jrp.2010.07.002.

Iacoboni, M., Lieberman, M. D., Knowlton, B. J., Molnar-Szakacs, I., Moritz, M., Throop, C. J., & Fiske, A. P. (2004). Watching social interactions produces dorsomedial prefrontal and medial parietal BOLD fMRI signal increases compared to a resting baseline. *NeuroImage, 21,* 1167–1173.

Jackson, P. L., & Decety, J. (2004). Motor cognition: A new paradigm to study self-other interactions. *Current Opinion in Neurobiology, 14,* 259–263.

Jacobson, E. (1964). *The self and the object world.* New York, NY: International Universities Press.

Jolie (n.d.). *Personal stories of dissociation: Depersonalization disorder.* Available at: http://www.angelfire.com/home/bphoenix1/disspers.html.

Jung, C. G. (1934–1954). *The archetypes and the collective unconscious* (1981, 2nd ed.). In *Collected Works* (vol. 9, Part 1). Princeton, NJ: Bollingen.

Kabat-Zinn, J. (1990). *Full catastrophe living: Using the wisdom of your body and mind to face stress, pain, and illness.* New York, NY: Dell.

Kagan, R. (1982). *The developing self.* Cambridge, MA: Harvard University Press.

Kandel, E. R. (2012). *The age of insight: The quest to understand the unconscious in art, mind, and brain: From Vienna 1900 to the present.* New York, NY: Random House.

Kendler, K. S., Aggen, S. H., Czajkowski, N., Røysamb, E., Tambs, K., Torgersen, S., Neale, M., & Reichborn-Kjennerud, T. (2008). The structure of genetic and environmental risk factors for DSM-IV personality disorders: A multivariate twin study. *Archives of General Psychiatry, 65(12),* 1438–1446.

Kernberg, O. F. (1967). Borderline personality organization. *Journal of the American Psychoanalytic Association, 15,* 641–675.

Kernberg, O. F. (1975). *Borderline conditions and pathological narcissism.* Northvale, NJ: Jason Aronson.

Kernberg, O. F. (1976). *Object relations theory and clinical psychoanalysis.* New York, NY: Jason Aronson.

Kernberg, O. F. (1982). Self, ego, affects, and drives. *Journal of American Psychoanalytic Association, 30,* 893–917.

Kernberg, O. F. (1992). *Aggression in personality disorders and perversions.* New Haven, CT: Yale University Press.

Kernberg, O. F. (2000). A concerned critique of psychoanalytic education. *International Journal of Psychoanalysis, 81,* 97–120.

Kernberg, O. F. (2009). Narcissistic personality disorders. *Psychiatric Annals, 39,* 106–110.

Kihlstrom, J. F. (1987). The cognitive unconscious. *Science, 237(4821),* 1445–1452.

Kihlstrom, J. F., & Cantor, N. (1984). Mental representations of the self. In L. Berkowitz, (Ed.), *Advances in experimental social psychology* (pp. 1–47). Orlando, FL: Academic Press.

Kirsch, P., Esslinger, C., Chen, Q., Mier, D., Lis, S., Siddhanti, S., Gruppe, H., Mattay, V. S., Gallhofer, B., & Lindenberg, A. (2005). Oxytocin modulates neural circuitry for social cognition and fear in humans. *Journal of Neuroscience, 25,* 11484–11493.

Klein, M. (1948). On the theory of anxiety and guilt. In *The Writings of Melanie Klein* (vol. 3, pp. 25–42). London: Virago.

Klein, M. (1957). *Envy and gratitude.* London: Tavistock. (Reprinted in the volume entitled *"Envy and gratitude"* in Klein's *Collected Works* published by Virago.)

Klein, M., & Spillius, E. B. (1988). *Mainly theory.* London: Routledge.

Kluft, R. P. (1984). Treatment of multiple personality disorder: A study of 33 cases. *Psychiatric Clinics of North America, 7(1),* 9–29.

Kluft, R. P. (1985). The natural history of multiple personality disorder. In R. P. Kluft (Ed.), *Childhood antecedents of multiple personality* (pp. 197–238). Washington, DC: American Psychiatric Press.

Kluft, R. P., & Fine, C. G. (1993). *Clinical perspectives on multiple personality disorder.* Washington, DC: American Psychiatric Press.

Klug, G., & Huber, D. (2009). Psychic structure: Exploring an empirically still unknown territory. *Journal of the American Psychoanalytic Association, 57(1),* 149–173.

Kohut, H. (1971). *Analysis of the self.* New York, NY: International Universities Press.

Kohut, H. (1972). Thoughts on narcissism and narcissistic rage. *Psychoanalytic Studies of the Child, 27,* 360–400.

Kohut, H. (1977). *The restoration of the self.* New York, NY: International Universities Press.

Kroger, J. (2007). *Identity development: Adolescence through adulthood* (2nd ed.). Newbury Park, CA: Sage.

Krupnick, J. L. (2001) Interpersonal psychotherapy for PTSD after interpersonal trauma. *Directions in Psychiatry, 20,* 237–253.

Kunzendorf, R. G. (2011). Depression, unlike normal sadness, is associated with a "flatter" self-perception and a "flatter" phenomenal world. *Imagination, Cognition, and Personality, 30(4),* 447–461.

Leary, M. R., & Tangney, J. P. (2003). The self as an organizing construct in the social and behavioral sciences. In M. R. Leary, & J. P. Tangney (Eds.), *Handbook of self and identity* (pp. 3–14). New York, NY: Guilford Press.

Levinson, D. J., & Levinson, J. D. (1997). *The seasons of a woman's life.* New York, NY: Ballantine Books.

Levinson, S. C. (1996). Language and space. *Annual Review of Anthropology, 25,* 353–382.

Lewis, H. B. (1971). *Shame and guilt in neurosis.* New York, NY: International Universities Press.

Lewis, T., Amini, F., & Lannon, R. (2000). *A general theory of love.* New York, NY: Random House.

Lichtenberg, J. (1975). The development of the sense of self. *Journal of American Psychoanalytic Association, 23,* 453–484.

Lichtenberg, J. (1983). *Psychoanalysis and infant research.* Hillsdale NJ: Analytic Press.

Linehan, M. M. (1993). *Skills training manual for treating borderline personality disorder.* New York, NY: Guilford Press.

Loewald, H. W. (1962). Internalization, separation, mourning, and the superego. *Psychoanalytic Quarterly, 31,* 483–504.

Loewenstein, R. J. (1991). An office mental status examination for complex chronic dissociative symptoms and multiple personality disorder. *The Psychiatric Clinics of North America, 14(3),* 567–604.

Luborsky, L., & Crits-Christoph, P. (1990) *Understanding transference: The Core Conflictual Relationship Theme method.* New York, NY: Basic Books.

Luborsky, L., Popp, C., & Barber, J. P. (1994). Common and special factors in different transference-related measures. *Psychotherapy Research, 4,* 172–183.

Luyten, P., & Blatt, S. (2013). Interpersonal relatedness and self-definition in normal and disrupted personality development. *American Psychologist, 68(3),* 172–183.

Mahler, M. S. (1968) *On human symbiosis and the vicissitudes of individuation.* With M. Furer. New York, NY: International Universities Press.

Main, M. (Ed.). (1975). *Mother-avoiding babies.* Paper presented at biennial meeting of Society for Research in Child Development.

Main, M., Hesse, E., & Kaplan, N. (2005). Predictability of attachment behavior and representational processes at 1, 6, and 18 years of age: The Berkeley Longitudinal Study. In K. E. Grossmann, K. Grossmann, & E. Waters (Eds.), *Attachment from infancy to adulthood* (pp. 245–304). New York, NY: Guilford Press.

Main, M., & Solomon, J. (1990). Procedures for identifying infants as disorganized/ disoriented during the Ainsworth Strange Situation. In M. T. Greenberg, D. Cicchetti, & E. M. Cummings (Eds.), *Attachment during the preschool years: Theory, research and intervention* (pp. 121–160). Chicago: University of Chicago Press.

Marmar, C., & Horowitz, M. J. (1986). Phenomenological analysis of splitting. *Psychotherapy, 23(1)*, 21-29.

Martin, J. R. (1997). Mindfulness: A proposed common factor. *Journal of Psychotherapy Integration, 7*, 291–312.

Masterson, J. (1980). *From borderline adolescent to functioning adult.* New York, NY: Wiley Interscience.

McWilliams, N. (2011). *Psychoanalytic diagnosis: Understanding personality structure in the clinical process* (2nd ed.). New York, NY: Guilford Press.

Mellon, R. (1998). Outsight: Radical behaviorism in psychotherapy. *Journal of Psychotherapy Integration, 8*, 123–146.

Millon, T. (1981). *Disorders of personality.* New York, NY: Wiley.

Millon, T. (1999). Reflections on psychosynergy: A model for integrating science, theory, classification, assessment, and therapy. *Journal of Personality Assessment, 72(3)*, 437–456.

Modell, A. (1984). *Psychoanalysis in a new context.* New York, NY: IUP.

Moran, J. M., Kelley, W. M., & Heatherton, T. F. (2013). What can the organization of the brain's default mode network tell us about self-knowledge? *Frontiers in Human Neuroscience, 7*, 1–6.

Morey, L. C., Shea, M. T., Markowitz, J. C., Stout, R. L, Hopwood, C. J., Gunderson, J. G., Grilo, C.M., McGlashan, T. H., Yen, S., Sanislow, C. A., & Skodol, A. E. (2010). State effects of major depression on the assessment of personality and personality disorder. *American Journal of Psychiatry, 167(5)*, 528–535.

Morishita, Y., & Aihara, K. (2004). Noise-reduction through interaction in gene expression and biochemical reaction processes. *Journal of Theoretical Biology, 228*, 315–325.

Muenchberger, H., Kendall, E., & Neal, R. (2008). Identity transition following traumatic brain injury: A dynamic process of contraction, expansion and tentative balance. *Brain Injury, 22(12)*, 979–992.

Mullin, A. S., & Hilsenroth, M. J. (2012). Relationship between patient pre-treatment object relations functioning and psychodynamic techniques early in treatment. *Clinical Psychology and Psychotherapy.* doi: 10.1002/cpp.1826.

Northoff, G., & Bermpohl, F. (2004). Cortical midline structures and the self. *Trends in Cognitive Science, 8(3)*, 102–107.

Northoff, G., Heinzel, A., de Greck, M., Bermpohl, F., Dobrowolny, H., & Panksepp, J. (2005). Self-referential processing in our brain: A meta-analysis of imaging studies on the self. *NeuroImage, 31*, 440–457.

Ofen, N. (2012). The development of neural correlates of memory formation. *Neuroscience & Biobehavioral Reviews, 36(7)*, 1708–1717.

Ogden, T. H. (1992). *The primitive edge of experience.* London: Jason Aronson.

Olausson, H., Charron, J., Marchand, S., Villemure, C., Strigo, I. A., & Bushnell, M. C. (2005). Feelings of warmth correlate with neural activity in right anterior insular cortex. *Neuroscience Letters, 389(1)*, 1–5.

Overall, J., & Gorham, D. (1962). The brief psychiatric rating scale. *Psychological Reports, 10*, 799.

Overall, N. C., Simpson, J. A., & Struthers, H. (2013). Buffering attachment-related avoidance: Softening emotional and behavioral defenses during conflict discussions. *Journal of Personality and Social Psychology, 104,* 854–871.

Oxford English Dictionary (2012). Self (7th ed.). Oxford: Oxford University Press.

Pally, R. (2000). *The mind–brain relationship.* New York, NY: Other Press.

Pally, R. (2007). The predicting brain: Unconscious repetition, conscious reflection, and therapeutic change; *International Journal of Psychoanalysis, 88 (Pt 4),* 861–881.

Panksepp, J. (2011). The "Dynamic Unconscious" may be experienced: Can we discuss unconscious emotions when there are no adequate measures of affective change? *Neuropsychoanalysis, 13,* 1.

Parkin, A. (1980). On masochistic enthrallment: A contribution to the study of moral masochism. *International Journal of Psychoanalysis, 61,* 307–314.

Parra, A. (2009). Out-of-body experiences and hallucinatory experiences: A psychological approach. *Imagination, Cognition and Personality, 29(3),* 211–223.

Pennebaker, J. W., & Francis, M. E. (1999). *Linguistic inquiry and word count: LIWC.* Hillsdale, NJ: Erlbaum Publishers.

Piaget, J. (1962). *Play, dreams and imitation in childhood.* New York, NY: Norton.

Piaget, J. (1967). *The child's conception of the world* (J. A. Tomlinson, trans.). London: Routledge & Kegan Paul.

Piaget, J., & Inhelder, B. (1969). *The psychology of the child.* New York, NY: Basic Books.

Piper, W. E., Azim, H. F. A., Joyce, A. S., & McCallum, M. (1991a). Transference interpretations, therapeutic alliance, and outcome in short-term individual psychotherapy. *Archives of General Psychiatry, 48(10),* 946–953.

Piper, W. E., Azim, H. F. A., Joyce, A. S., McCallum, M., Nixon, G. W. H., & Segal, P. S. (1991b). Quality of object relations versus interpersonal functioning as predictors of therapeutic alliance and psychotherapy outcome. *Journal of Nervous & Mental Disease, 179,* 432–438.

Piper, W. E., Joyce, A. S., McCallum, M., & Azim, H. F. A. (1993). Concentration and correspondence of transference interpretations in short-term psychotherapy. *Journal of Consulting and Clinical Psychology, 61(4),* 586–595.

Platek, S. M., Keenan, J. P., Gallup, G. G., & Feroze, B. (2004). Where am I? The neurological correlates of self and other. *Cognitive Brain Research, 19,* 114–122.

Plomin, R., DeFries, J. C., McClearn, G. E., & McGuffin, P. (2008). *Behavioral genetics.* New York, NY: Worth Publishers.

Prigerson, H. G., Horowitz, M. J., Jacobs, S. C., Parkes, C. M., Aslan, M., Goodkin, K., Raphael, B., et al. (2012). Prolonged grief disorder: Psychometric validation of criteria proposed for DSM-V and ICD-11. *PLOS Medicine,* available at: http://www.plosmedicine.org/article/info%3Adoi%2F10.1371%2Fjournal.pmed.1000121;jsessionid=4ED1 FA2260A0EF5C70A09022DBEAA23D.

Putnam, F. W. (1999). Pierre Janet and modern views of dissociation. In M. J. Horowitz (Ed.), *Essential papers on posttraumatic stress disorder* (pp. 116–135). New York, NY: New York University Press.

Rameson, L. T., Satpute, A. B., & Lieberman, M. D. (2010). The neural correlates of implicit and explicit self-relevant processing. *NeuroImage, 50,* 701–708.

Rasch, B., Spalek, K., Buholzer, S., Luechinger, R., Boesiger, P., Papassotiropoulos, A., & De Quervain, D. J-F. (2009). A genetic variation of the noradrenergic system is related to differential amygdala activation during encoding of emotional memories.

Proceedings of the National Academy of Sciences of the United States of America,
106(45), 19191–19196.

Ronningstam, E. (2009). Narcissistic personality disorder: Facing DSM-V. *Psychiatric Annals, 39,* 111–123.

Rotheram-Borus, M. J., & Fernandez, M. I. (1995). Sexual orientation and developmental challenges experienced by gay and lesbian youth. *Journal of Adolescence, 12,* 361–374.

Rotheram-Borus, M. J., & Langabeer, K. A. (2001). Developmental trajectories of gay, lesbian, and bisexual youths. In A. R. D'Angell, & C. J. Patterson (Eds.), *Lesbian, gay, and bisexual identities in youth.* New York, NY: Oxford University Press.

Rothstein, A. (1984). The fear of humiliation. *Journal of the American Psychoanalytic Association, 32,* 99–116.

Rummelhart, D. E., & McClellan, J. L. (1986). *Parallel distributed processing.* Cambridge, MA: MIT Press.

Russ, E., Shedler, J., Bradley, R., & Westen, D. (2008). Refining the construct of narcissistic personality disorder: Diagnostic criteria and subtypes. *American Journal of Psychiatry, 165,* 1473–1481.

Ryle, A. (1997). The structure and development of borderline personality disorder: A proposed model. *British Journal of Psychiatry, 170,* 82.

Sandler, C. M. (1960) The background of safety. *International Journal of Psychoanalysis, 41,* 352–356.

Sandler, J., & Rosenblatt, B. (1962). *The concept of the representational world.* New York, NY: International Universities Press.

Sandler, J., & Sandler, A.-M. (1997). A psychoanalytic theory of repression and unconscious. In J. Sandler, & P. Fonagy (Eds.), *Recovered memories of abuse: True or false?* Monograph series of the Psychoanalysis Unit of University College, London and the Anna Freud Centre, No. 2 (pp. 162–181). Madison, CT: International Universities Press, Inc.

Schore, A. N., & Schore, A. N. (2003). *Affect dysregulation and disorders of the self: Affect regulation and the repair of the self.* New York, NY: W.W. Norton.

Searles, H. F. (1986). Dual- and multiple-identity processes in ego-functioning. In *My work with borderline patients* (pp. 79–97). Northvale, NJ: Jason Aronson.

Segal, Z. (2004). *Mindfulness-based cognitive behavioral therapy.* Washington, DC: American Psychological Association.

Semendefer, K., Armstrong, E., Schleicher, A., Zilles, K., & Hoesen, G. (2001). Prefrontal cortex in humans and apes: A comparative study of area 10. *American Journal of Physical Anthropology, 114(3),* 224–241.

Shear, K., Frank, E., Houck, P., & Reynolds, C. (2005).Treatment of complicated grief: A randomized controlled trial. *Journal of the American Medical Association, 293,* 2601–2608.

Sheldon, K. M., Ryan, R. M., Rawsthorne, L. J., & Hardi, B. (1997). Core self and true self: Cross-role variation in the Big-Five Personality Traits and its relations with psychological authenticity and subjective well-being. *Journal of Personality and Social Psychology, 73(6),* 1380–1393.

Shestyuk, A. Y., & Deldin, P. J. (2010). Automatic and strategic representation of the self in major depression: Trait and state abnormalities. *American Journal of Psychiatry, 167(5),* 536–544.

Shweder, R. A. (1991). *Thinking through cultures.* Cambridge, MA: Harvard University Press.

Siegel, S. (2010). The contents of perception. In *The Stanford encyclopedia of philosophy.* Stanford, CA: Stanford University Press.

Singer, J. L. (1974). *Imagery and daydream methods in psychotherapy and behavior modification*. New York, NY: Academic Press.

Skodol, A. E., Clark, L. A., Bender, D. S., Krueger, R. F., Money, L. C., Verheul, R., & Oldham, J. M. (2011a). Proposed changes in personality and personality disorder assessment and diagnosis for DSM-5, part I: Description and rationale. *Personality Disorders: Theory, Research and Treatment, 2*, 4–22.

Skodol, A. E., Clark, L. A., Bender, D. S., Krueger, R. F., Money, L. C., Verheul, R., & Oldham, J. M. (2011b). Proposed changes in personality and personality disorder assessment and diagnosis for DSM-5, part II: Clinical application. *Personality Disorders: Theory, Research and Treatment, 2*, 23–40.

Slaughter, A. M. (2012). Why women still can't have it all. *The Atlantic Monthly*. Available at: http://www.theatlantic.com/magazine/archive/2012/07/why-women-still-can-8217-t-have-it-all/9020/1/.

Sophie, J. (1985–86). A critical examination of stage theories of lesbian identity development. *Journal of Homosexuality, 12*, 39–51.

Sperling, W. H., & Berman, M. B. (1991) Parental attachment and emotional distress in the transition to college. *Journal of Youth and Adolescence, 20(4)*, 427–440.

Sperry, R. W. (1974) Lateral specialization in the surgically separated hemispheres. In F. Schmitt, & F. Worden (Eds.), *Neurosciences Third Study Program* (Ch. I, vol. 3, pp. 5–19). Cambridge, MA: MIT Press.

Srouf, A., & Fleeson, J. (1986). Attachment and the construction of relationships. In W. Hartup, & Z. Rubin (Eds.), *Relationships and development*. Hillsdale, NJ: Lawrence Erlbaum.

Sroufe, L. A. (1979). The coherence of individual development: Early care attachment, and subsequent developmental issues. *American Psychologist, 34*, 834–841.

Steele, C. M. (1988). The psychology of self-affirmation: Sustaining the integrity of the self. In L. Berkowitz (Ed.), *Advances in experimental social psychology* (vol. 21, pp. 181–227). San Diego, CA: Academic Press.

Steinberg, L., & Silverberg, S. B. (1986). The vicissitudes of autonomy in early adolescence. *Child Development, 57(4)*, 841–851.

Steinberg, M., Cicchetti, D. V., Buchanan, J., Hall, P. E., & Rounsaville, B. J. (1993). Clinical assessment of dissociative symptoms and disorders: The structured clinical interview for DSM-IV dissociative disorders (SCID-D). *Dissociation, VI(1)*, 3–15.

Steiner, J. (1993). *Psychic retreats: Pathological organisations in psychotic, neurotic, and borderline patients*. London: Routledge.

Steiner, J. (1994). Patient-centered and analyst-centered interpretations: Some implications of containment and countertransference. *Psychoanalytic Inquiry, 14*, 406–422.

Stern, D. N. (1985). *The interpersonal world of the infant*. New York, NY: Basic Books.

Stern, D. N. (2004). *The present moment in psychotherapy and everyday life*. New York, NY: W.W. Norton.

Stinson, C. H., & Horowitz, M. J. (1993). Psyclops: An exploratory graphical system for clinical research and education. *Psychiatry, 56*, 375–389.

Stolorow, R. D., & Lachmann, F. M. (1980). *The psychoanalysis of developmental arrests*. New York, NY: International Universities Press.

Strauman, T. J., & Higgins, E. T. (1987). Automatic activation of self discrepancies and emotional syndromes: When cognitive structures influence affect. *Journal of Personality & Social Psychology, 53*, 1004–1014.

Strauss, A. L., & Corbin, J. M. (1990). *Basics of qualitative research: Grounded theory procedures and techniques*. Newbury Park, CA: Sage Publications.

Strupp, H. H. (1980). Success and failure in time-limited psychotherapy: Further evidence. *Archives of General Psychiatry, 37,* 947–954.

Strupp, H. H. (1993). The Vanderbilt psychotherapy studies: Synopsis. *Journal of Consulting and Clinical Psychology, 61,* 431–433.

Tedeschi, R. G., & Calhoun, L. G. (1996). The posttraumatic growth inventory: Measuring the positive legacy of trauma. *Journal of Traumatic Stress, 9(3),* 455–471.

Thomas, A., Chess, S., & Birch, H. G. (1968). *Temperament and behavior disorders in children.* New York, NY: New York University Press.

Tracy, J. L., Cheng, J. T., Robina, R. W., & Trzesniewski, K. H. (2009). Authentic and hubristic pride: The affective core of self-esteem and narcissism. *Self and Identity, 8(2–3),* 196–213. Doi:10.1080/15298860802505053.

Troiden, R. R. (1988). Homosexual identity development. *Journal of Adolescent Health Care, 9,* 105–113.

Ullrich, P. M., Lutgendorf, S. K., Stapleton, J. T., & Horowitz, M. J. (2004). Self regard and concealment of homosexuality as predictors of CD4+ cell count over time among HIV seropositive gay men. *Psychology & Health, 19(2),* 183–196.

Vaillant, G. E. (1994). Ego mechanisms of defense and personality psychopathology. *Journal of Abnormal Psychology, 102(1),* 44–50.

Vaillant, G. E. (2012). Youth purpose among the "greatest generation." *The Journal of Positive Psychology, 7(4).*

Vaillant, N. G. (2004). Discrimination in matchmaking: Evidence from the price policy of a French marriage bureau. *Applied Economics, 36,* 723–729.

Vasconcellos, J. (n.d.). The Vasconcellos Project. Available at: www.politicsoftrust.net.

Vasire, S., & Wilson, T. D. (2012). *Handbook of self-knowledge.* New York, NY: Guilford Press.

Washington, J. (2012). What's an American Indian? Warren case stirs query. Available at: http://heraldnet.com/article/20120526/NEWS02/705269950.

Watson, L. A., Dritschel, B., Obonsawin, M. C., & Jentzsch, I. (2007). Seeing yourself in a positive light: Brain correlates of the self-positivity bias. *Brain Research, 1152(4),* 106–110.

Westen, D. (2007). *Political brain: The role of emotion in deciding the fate of the nation.* New York, NY: New York Public Affairs.

Winnicott, D. W. (1958). The capacity to be alone. *International Journal of Psychoanalysis, 39,* 416–420.

Wood, A. M., Linley, P. A., Maltby, J., Baliousis, M., & Joseph, S. (2008). The authentic personality: A theoretical and empirical conceptualization and the development of the authenticity scale. *Journal of Counseling Psychology, 55(3),* 385–399.

Wurmser, L. (1981). *The mask of shame.* Baltimore, MD: Johns Hopkins University Press.

Young, J. E., Klosko, J. S., & Weishaar, M. E. (2003). *Schema therapy: A practitioner's guide.* New York, NY: Guilford Press.

Young, L., Bechara, A., Tranel, D., Damasio, H., Hauser, M., & Damasio, A. (2010). Damage to ventromedial prefrontal cortex impairs judgment of harmful intent, *Neuron, 65(6),* 845–851.

Zelner, M. (2011). The neural basis of the dynamic unconscious. *Neuropsychoanalysis, 13(1),* 5.

Zimmerman, M., Morgan, T. A., Chelminski, I., Young, D., & Dalrymple, K. (2012). Differences between older and younger adults with Borderline Personality Disorder on clinical presentation and impairment. *Journal of Psychiatric Research, 47(10),* 1507–1513.

Index